D1729958

SWISS SUPPERS

52 WHOLESOME RECIPES
FROM THE HEART OF EUROPE

Swiss Suppers
52 Wholesome Recipes from the Heart of Europe

Author: Heddi Nieuwsma
Photography: Dorian Rollin
Historical photos on p. 10 and 32: Swiss National Library,
Federal Archives of Historic Monuments: Archiv Photoglob–Wehrli
Food Styling: Camille Stoos
Graphic Design & Illustrations: Jagna Pilczuk
Editing: Leah Witton
Proofreading: Karin Waldhauser

ISBN: 978–3–03964–058–4

First edition: October 2024
Deposit copy in Switzerland: October 2024
First International Edition: 2025
Printed in the Czech Republic

© 2024 HELVETIQ (Helvetiq SA)
Mittlere Strasse 4
CH–4056 Basel
Switzerland

helvetiq.com

MIX
Paper from
responsible sources
FSC® C014138

HEDDI NIEUWSMA
DORIAN ROLLIN

SWISS SUPPERS

52 WHOLESOME RECIPES FROM THE HEART OF EUROPE

TABLE OF CONTENTS

A Sampling of Swiss Suppers by Region

The list of recipes in this book by geographic area (p. 247) as well as the maps next to each recipe, indicate what is generally considered their place of origin or where you will most likely find them today. Of course, boundaries for these dishes are certainly fluid, especially over time, and some exist in multiple regions of the country, but perhaps with a different name.

SCHNETZ OND HÄPPERE
P. 85

BÄRNER CHÄSCHÜECHLI
P. 199

JACQUERIE
NEUCHÂTELOISE
REVISITÉE
P. 145

PÔCHOUSE DU LÉMAN
P. 27

SOUPE DU CHALET
P. 31

FONDUE À LA TOMATE
P. 69

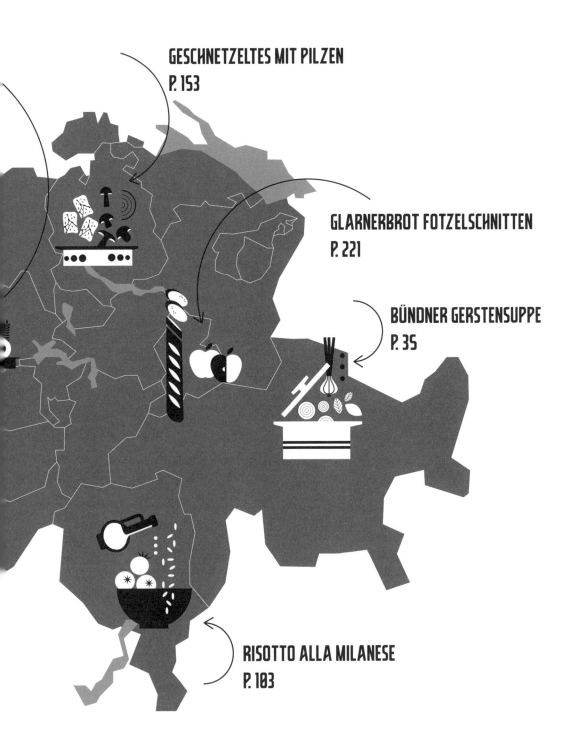

GESCHNETZELTES MIT PILZEN
P. 153

GLARNERBROT FOTZELSCHNITTEN
P. 221

BÜNDNER GERSTENSUPPE
P. 35

RISOTTO ALLA MILANESE
P. 103

Getting hungry?
Keep reading to discover 52 supper recipes from across Switzerland.

I. INTRODUCTION

Do you need some help planning what to make for supper?
Would you like to learn more about Swiss cuisine and traditions?
Are you looking for culinary destinations to visit in Switzerland?

Swiss Suppers brings you a collection of 52 comforting supper ideas inspired by traditional dishes from Switzerland—fresh, simple and delicious recipes for your evening meal. More than just a cookbook, every recipe comes with a story about its origin and ingredients, and where to find it in this Alpine country. This book also gives you insider tips for food events and destinations. I want to help you discover Switzerland through its culinary landscape.

These recipes are shaped by more than a decade of experience cooking at home in the French-speaking part of Switzerland and traveling throughout the country. I have included some national favorites, such as Rösti (p. 81) and fondue (p. 69), but you will also find some very regional specialties. For example, visiting the Italian-speaking region of Valposchiavo led to my recipe for Capunet (p. 115). I serve these little spinach dumplings in a roasted tomato sauce, sprinkled with fresh basil and grated Sbrinz cheese. From the canton of Neuchâtel, comes a recipe for Steak Vigneron (p. 165). This popular seasoned ground beef sandwich can be enjoyed at local festivals in the fall, such as the Fête des Vendanges (wine harvest festival). Even if you grew up in Switzerland, there is a good chance you will come across a Swiss dish in this book that you have never heard of before.

While I was writing and baking for my first two cookbooks, *Swiss Bread* (2020) and *Sweet + Swiss* (2022), my husband and I still had to make supper! Every night when I was tired and covered in flour, we opened the refrigerator door and contemplated our options. *Swiss Suppers* is the book I needed then—a guide to easy recipes with wholesome ingredients, make-ahead tips and interesting Swiss stories.

WHAT MAKES SWISS FOOD UNIQUE?

The uniqueness of Swiss cuisine is due in part to the diversity of its linguistic regions—this small country has four national languages: German, French, Italian and Romansh. The cultural differences among these regions mean that there is a wide variety of traditional dishes on offer. Within a day, you could travel around the country and feast on Swiss Italian saffron risotto (p. 103), Swiss French Fricassée Genevoise (p. 133) and Swiss German Ofeturli (p. 77). Given this diversity, only a small number of dishes make up what might be considered Switzerland's national cuisine, such as a braided loaf of Zopf for Sunday breakfast. In this book, I try to give you a varied perspective on Swiss food by incorporating recipes and stories from all corners of the country.

At its core, Swiss cuisine has always emphasized local and seasonal ingredients. What started out of necessity, with people living in rural communities and isolated mountainous regions, corresponds to sustainable practices for today—eating fewer processed foods, reducing packaging and shortening the distance our food travels to reach us. A number of the tried-and-true recipes in this book also help reduce food waste by using up your leftover pieces of cheese or old bread.

Young men and women in Bernese costume, approx. 1910

WHAT IS A TRADITIONALLY SWISS SUPPER?

Znacht (Swiss German) / **souper** (French) / **cena** (Italian) / **Tschaina** (Romansh)

The chapters of this book feature the types of dishes found in Switzerland: soup, potatoes, rice, pasta, dumplings, stews and savory tarts. There is also a chapter with options for sweet suppers, often considered a more Swiss German custom. As you may have guessed already, the stereotype is true: cheese factors heavily in Swiss cuisine, along with other dairy products. In addition, lake fish, sausage and dried meats are used in nearly all regions of the country.

When I ask people about Swiss suppers, they inevitably bring up *café complet*. This term describes what some might consider to be an old-fashioned meal of coffee with milk served with cold dishes. Bread has remained an essential part of this meal, along with cheese, cold cuts, butter and jam. This way of eating has survived for over a century in Switzerland, with the first use of the term seen in the late 19th century in hotel advertisements. It still features in the menus of some Swiss hospitals today. While people like *café complet* for its simplicity, others complain that it often lacks fruit and vegetables.

Swiss suppers have, of course, evolved over time. For previous generations, the noontime meal would generally be a larger affair than supper, and it was more common to return home from work for lunch. If you live in Switzerland, you know that the majority of Swiss public schools do not serve lunch, and children go home or to a childcare facility at midday. Nowadays, more people eat lunch away from home than in the past. As such, supper is often the time when a family or household can finally enjoy a meal together around the same table.

Let us also keep in mind that Switzerland is made up of people from around the world. The Swiss government reports that about 40% of the population in 2022 had a migration background. This means that Swiss cuisine can have influences from other countries and not only from its neighbors—Germany, France, Italy, Austria and Lichtenstein—but from places further afield. Certainly, this is true for my household, where we inject some American flavor into our Swiss cooking—like adding sweet potatoes to the Guyenëfles from Valais (p. 123).

WHY IS AN AMERICAN WRITING A BOOK ABOUT SWISS SUPPERS?

Like many people, I have always loved food and cooking, but when I arrived in Switzerland, I finally had the time to really study it. Having left my job in Boston, I was now taking care of my young children full-time and routinely preparing three meals a day. And, I had a whole new array of ingredients and dishes to discover! My neighborhood had several butchers, a cheesemonger, bakeries with bread and pastries made onsite, and chocolatiers, including one of the oldest operating in Switzerland. In two minutes, I could walk to the farmers' market, held two or three times a week, with the most beautiful fresh produce. I took a deep dive into learning about my newly adopted home through its food.

Always in search of a new regional recipe, I have traveled to all 26 of Switzerland's cantons (similar to states). Every chance I get, I search through cookbooks and talk with everyone I can about Swiss food. I now have over a decade of first-hand experience in the land of chocolate and cheese, and writing for my blog, *Cuisine Helvetica* since 2015. This work has given me some incredible experiences—dining at mountain restaurants, interviewing Michelin-starred chefs, serving as a jury member for food competitions, taking and teaching cooking classes and attending culinary events throughout the country.

Over time, I started to be recognized for my work, for which I am incredibly grateful. The American magazine *Saveur* selected *Cuisine Helvetica* as a 2018 finalist for the "Best Special Interest" category as part of its annual blog awards, and I attended the ceremony in Memphis, Tennessee. In 2020, following the publication of my first book, *Swiss Bread*, Radiotelevisione svizzera (the Swiss Italian TV station) interviewed me for their nightly news program. Most recently, my second book, *Sweet + Swiss*, won the 2023 Swiss Gourmet Book Award "Gold Category" for dessert and pastry.

Above all, I am a self-taught cook and baker, and I develop my recipes for home cooks like me who do not always have much time or patience for cooking. I always strive to write accessible recipes for dishes that you will want to make again and again.

HOW DID I DEVELOP THESE RECIPES?

I generally started with a broad review of recipes for a particular dish, such as Stunggis, a pork stew from Nidwalden (p. 137). Then, I tried to talk with people who had experience making the dish, watched archival videos or traveled to places where I could taste the real thing for myself. Over the years, I have visited bakeries in Geneva, Alpine pastures in Obwalden and remote valleys in Ticino, among other locations, to try and bring their flavors to the pages of this book. I have included stories with my recipes to encourage you to visit these extraordinary places for yourself. For a complete list of my sources and references for this book, you will find a link on my blog.

After my initial research phases, I sat down and wrote my own recipes, taking into consideration my favorite flavor combinations and textures, as well as ease of preparation. These supper ideas reflect my own interpretation of these Swiss dishes. Each recipe has been tested multiple times by me and at least one independent tester. I really want these recipes to work for you!

I have loved pulling together this collection of recipes. It is my sincere wish that these Swiss supper recipes help you connect (or reconnect) with Switzerland and learn a little bit about its history, culture and geography. Just as important, I hope this book gives you some new ideas for suppertime.

From my kitchen to yours, *En Guetä* (Swiss German), *Bon appétit* (French), *Buon appetito* (Italian) and *Bun appetit* (Romansh),

Heddi Nieuwsma
cuisinehelvetica.com

II. GETTING STARTED

To help you navigate through the recipes in this book, I have prepared some notes for you. The sections in this chapter discuss in more detail the ingredients I use, as well as substitutions. You will also find some foundational recipes, such as herbed croutons (p. 21), vegetable stock (p. 19) and two common Swiss salad dressings (p. 20–21).

A. MEASURING INGREDIENTS

Each recipe has measurements by weight (grams, ounces), volume (milliliters, cups, teaspoons or tablespoons) or both. Weighing the ingredients will give you the most accurate results. As an American, all my previous experience with recipes involved measurement by volume. When I moved to Switzerland, I bought my very first cooking scale!

B. OVEN

The baking temperatures for my recipes are for a conventional electric oven with top and bottom heat. If you have a convection oven, you will need to reduce the baking time by about 25% or the temperature by 15°C (25°F). Please check the instructions for your oven to know which adjustments will achieve the best results.

C. KEY INGREDIENTS

DAIRY PRODUCTS

When I tested my recipes in my Swiss kitchen, these are the dairy products I used.

- **Milk:** For all my recipes, unless otherwise specified, I use milk with 2.5% milk fat.
- **Cream:** When recipes refer to "light cream," this product has a milk fat of 25%. For recipes with "heavy cream," the milk fat content is 35%.
- **Butter:** All the recipes in this book call for unsalted butter. If you are using salted butter, you may want to adjust the amount of salt in the recipe if it calls for a large quantity of unsalted butter. If you are in the US, I recommend using a European-style butter with a higher fat content for the bread and pastry recipes.
- **Cheese:** Switzerland has over 450 types of cheese! For accessibility, my recipes generally call for Swiss cheeses that are more well-known and relatively easy to find, such as Gruyère, Emmentaler and Raclette. However, I recommend experimenting with lots of different kinds of Swiss cheeses to determine which ones you like best.

FLOUR

Switzerland has a wealth of flour varieties and its own classification system based on the degree of grinding, also referred to as the extraction rate. A flour made only with the inner kernel from a grain of wheat has a lower degree of grinding. To help you find substitutions wherever you are, here are some details about flours in different countries.

Swiss Flour Types by Country

SWITZERLAND	FRANCE	GERMANY	UK	US
White flour Type 550 Weissmehl (DE) farine blanche (FR) farina bianca (IT) Degree of grinding: 0–65% Protein content: 12%	T55 farine tout usage OR farine blanche	Type 550 Weissmehl	plain flour OR strong white flour (for yeasted dough)	all-purpose flour OR bread flour (for yeasted dough)
Whole wheat flour Type 1900 Vollkornmehl (DE) farine complète (FR) farina integrale (IT) Degree of grinding: 98–100% Protein content: 14%	T150 farine complète OR farina integrale	Vollkornmehl	wholemeal flour	whole wheat flour

How American bakers convert one cup of all-purpose flour to grams differs greatly—I have seen amounts ranging from 120 to 142 grams. For recipes that call for a significant quantity of flour, this can have a large impact on the result.

Based on my tests here in Switzerland, and on those of my recipe testers in the US and the UK, I have used 125 grams for one cup of all-purpose flour for the recipes in this book. This conversion requires that you use the traditional spoon-and-level method when filling a measuring cup. First, you aerate the flour in its container by stirring it with a spoon. Next, you spoon the flour into the cup. Once the cup is overflowing with flour, you level it off with a knife.

YEAST

Four recipes in this book call for yeast: Speckkuchen (p.191), Gâteau du Cloître (p. 175), the bread rolls for Steak Vigneron (p. 165), and Glarnerbrot (p. 221). When I make these recipes in Switzerland, I use fresh organic yeast (sometimes referred to as cake yeast in the US). Each of these recipes, however, also provides the option to use dry yeast. When using dry yeast, make sure to read the package, so you know what kind you have. Active dry yeast may need to be activated in lukewarm water, while instant yeast can be added directly to the flour and other ingredients.

According to King Arthur Flour, an American baking company, you can calculate the amount of dry yeast to use by multiplying the amount of fresh yeast by 0.4 for active dry yeast, or by 0.33 for instant yeast.

One of the most important things to remember when using fresh yeast or yeast that needs activating is that the liquid you combine it with should only be lukewarm. I always test the temperature of the liquid first by touching it with my fingers. It should be at or just slightly warmer than body temperature.

BREADCRUMBS

You can make your own breadcrumbs with stale bread or you can buy them at the supermarket or at some bakeries. At home, I use an attachment for my mixer to make breadcrumbs, but you could also use a food processor. Depending on the texture of the bread, using a grater or crushing it with a rolling pin may also work for this task.

EGGS

I use large eggs with a weight of about 63 grams (about 2 ¼ ounces). In the US, these eggs would generally be considered "extra-large." For recipes in this book with a lot of eggs, such as the Rüebli–Quiche (p. 171) or the Apfelauflauf (p. 229), the total weight of the eggs is important. If you are using smaller eggs, you may need to adjust the recipe by adding an extra egg, for example.

CURED MEATS AND SAUSAGES

Before I moved to Switzerland, I had no idea that every region of this country has its own special sausage or cured meat. They range from the raw–cured pork saucissons in the French-speaking cantons to the pre-cooked veal St. Galler Bratwurst from the German-speaking canton of St. Gallen. The cervelat (or cervelas), widely considered to be Switzerland's national sausage, is part of the country's culinary heritage. Cut crosswise at its ends, skewered on a stick and cooked over a wood fire is a common way to enjoy this sausage, especially in the summer.

Switzerland also has a tradition of other types of cured meats. My recipe for Bündner Gerstensuppe (p. 35) calls for one of them—Bündnerfleisch, an air-dried and raw-cured beef. The seasoning mixture for this dried beef can include spices such as pepper, garlic, ginger, juniper, bay leaf and allspice.

Several of these sausages and cured meat products have been recognized with an *indication géographique protégée* (protected geographic indication) designation. This means that at least one step in the production process must take place in the product's designated region of origin with raw materials that are 100% Swiss. Some examples of products include *lard sec*, a type of dried bacon from the canton of Valais, and Mostbröckli, a smoked, dried cut of thigh or sirloin beef from the Appenzell region.

Very few recipes in this book call for traditional Swiss sausages and cured meats, as they are not always easy to find outside their region of origin. When I do use them, I make sure to offer substitutes.

FISH

I live about a 5-minute walk from Lac Neuchâtel—the largest lake entirely contained within Switzerland's borders. Bodensee (Lake Constance) and Lac Léman (Lake Geneva) are larger, but they are only partially located within the country. In the south, there is also Lago di Lugano (Lake Lugano) and Lago Maggiore. When you take into consideration all of Switzerland's various Alpine lakes, it should not be surprising that this small country has over 100 different fish species. To give you a taste of Swiss fish, I have included Pôchouse du Léman (p.27), a bouillabaisse-like recipe from the French-speaking part of Switzerland.

VEGETABLE STOCK

Numerous recipes in this book call for vegetable stock. Stock, broth and bouillon are terms that are sometimes used interchangeably. For the purposes of this book, I define stock as a seasoned, vegetable-laced liquid designed to add flavor to a dish but not generally consumed on its own. If I have time, I like to make it myself, using the recipe shown below. When I am in a hurry, I use an organic, vegan, powdered bouillon instead of my homemade liquid stock. Depending on the type you use, you may need to adjust the amount of salt.

HOMEMADE VEGETABLE STOCK

I was inspired to make my own vegetable stock after seeing the recipe for "Bouillon de légumes pour risotto" (vegetable bouillon for risotto) from Riz du Vully. Then, I had the chance to taste a delicious risotto made with the homemade bouillon (stock) of company co-owners Léandre and Johanna Guillod. The purpose of this stock is to serve as an ingredient for the recipes in this book, not as a soup to be eaten on its own.

Quantity: approx. 2 liters of stock (8 ½ cups)

Prep: 5–10 mins
Cook: 2 hrs

INGREDIENTS:

2 liters water (8 ½ cups)

1 large carrot, peeled and halved lengthwise

1 celery stalk, halved

1 onion, peeled and halved

1 leek, halved (optional)

handful fresh herbs (e.g., sage, parsley, thyme, rosemary)

15 g salt (2 ½ teaspoons)

INSTRUCTIONS:

1. Add all the ingredients to a large pot. Bring the mixture to a boil and then lower the temperature to a simmer. Cover the pot and let it continue to simmer for about 2 hours.

2. Let the mixture cool. Pour it through a sieve to remove all the solid ingredients. Use immediately or refrigerate the stock for up to 2–3 days.

D. SWISS SALADS

If you have ever spent time in Switzerland, you will know that one of the most common Swiss salads is a *Gemischter Salat* (German), *salad mêlée* or *mixte* (French) or *insalata mixta* (Italian). You will find this "mixed salad" on restaurant menus throughout the country. It will generally include a lettuce salad surrounded by a variety of other individual salads, including grated carrots, grated celery root, chopped roasted beets, corn, potato salad (p. 73) and more. When a restaurant pairs a mixed salad with a source of protein, such as a large pork schnitzel or a sliced chicken breast, they call it a Fitnessteller (fitness plate).

The *Wurstsalat* represents another typically Swiss "salad." You make this dish with chopped cervelat sausage and cheese, typically Gruyère or Emmentaler. Meat and cheese are the stars of this salad, which can also include chopped onions, radishes and boiled potatoes. My father-in-law ordered this at a mountain restaurant one time, only realizing after it arrived that there was no lettuce in sight!

One of my favorite Swiss salad greens, which I had never seen in the US, is *Nüsslisalat* (German), *doucette* or *rampon* (French), or *formentino* (Italian). In English, it is called lamb's lettuce or corn salad. The little leaves grow in bunches. Available primarily during the winter, *Nüsslisalat* is often served with hard-boiled eggs, bacon and croutons.

SALAD DRESSINGS

I used to routinely buy bottled salad dressings at the supermarket, but I finally switched to making my own. Here are two super easy recipes for two of the most common Swiss salad dressings: French Dressing and Italian Dressing. In the US, we use the term "French" to describe a sweetish, tomato-based sauce for salads. In Switzerland, the Sauce à salade française (French dressing) more closely resembles a thinner version of the American "ranch" dressing. Italian dressing refers to a vinaigrette, often made with red wine vinegar, but not exclusively.

FRENCH DRESSING
One of the most classic Swiss salad dressings.

Servings: 2–4

Prep: about 5 mins

INGREDIENTS:

4 tablespoons mayonnaise

1 tablespoon plain yogurt

2 tablespoons apple cider vinegar

1 tablespoon milk

1 clove garlic, minced

1 teaspoon dried basil

¼ teaspoon Dijon mustard

salt and pepper, to taste

INSTRUCTIONS:

Mix all the ingredients together until well combined. Store in a sealed container in the refrigerator for no more than 2–3 days.

ITALIAN DRESSING

A super simple vinaigrette that works with most any salad.

Servings: 4

Prep: 5–10 mins

INGREDIENTS:

6 tablespoons olive oil

2 tablespoons red wine vinegar

1 clove garlic, minced

½ teaspoon dried thyme

½ teaspoon dried oregano

¼ teaspoon honey

fresh parsley, finely chopped
(optional)

salt and pepper, to taste

INSTRUCTIONS:

Mix all the ingredients together until well combined. Store in a sealed container in the refrigerator for no more than 2-3 days.

HERBED CROUTONS

Rejuvenate your stale bread by turning it into croutons. You can put them on soups and salads, or like my family, snack on them as soon as they come out of the oven!

Servings: 4–6

Prep: about 15 mins
Bake: 10–15 mins

INGREDIENTS:

60 ml olive oil (¼ cup)

1–2 cloves garlic, minced

1 pinch chili flakes (optional)

250 g (about 4 cups)
stale bread, cubed

a handful of fresh herbs (e.g., cilantro, parsley, basil), finely chopped

INSTRUCTIONS:

1. Add the olive oil, garlic and chili flakes to a small frying pan. Simmer over medium-low heat for about 5 minutes. Do not let the garlic turn brown or burn.

2. Put the cubed bread in a large bowl. Drizzle half the olive oil mixture over the bread. Toss the bread cubes in the oil. Repeat with the remaining oil and continue tossing until the bread cubes are evenly coated in the oil. Add the chopped herbs to the bowl and stir until all the ingredients are well combined.

3. Bake in an oven heated to 180°C (350°F) for 10–15 minutes, depending on how crispy you like your croutons. Be careful not to overbake them, otherwise they will become too hard or burn. Let them cool completely and then store in a sealed container. Use within 2–3 days.

ARE YOU READY TO START MAKING SOME SWISS SUPPERS?

Now that we have covered some of the basics, you are ready to choose from the 52 recipes on the following pages!

To help you navigate through these recipes, please refer to the following symbols and the list on p. 246:

⟲ MAKE AHEAD:

To save time at the end of the day, these recipes have one or more steps you can tackle ahead of time. Some of these recipes can be made entirely in advance and reheated for supper.

⟳ SUPER FAST:

You can throw these recipes together quickly!

📅 WEEKEND:

These recipes have a few more steps or require a longer cooking time, so you may want to tackle them on the weekend, for example.

⊗ VEGETARIAN OPTION:

These recipes are either vegetarian as written or can be made vegetarian by omitting or replacing the meat in the recipe.

SOUPS

A nourishing bowl of soup at the end of the day has remained a popular Swiss supper for generations. The pot could simmer on the stove during the day while work was getting done. You could also revive stale bread by adding a slice to your bowl.

Every Swiss canton has their own popular soups and, in this chapter, I present you with a selection of my favorites. While some are well-known regional soups, such as Basler Mehlsuppe (flour soup, p. 39), I also wanted to provide some lesser-known regional soups, such as Bürbora (pumpkin soup, p. 43) from Ticino. Of course, one of the most common soups found in this Italian-speaking canton is minestrone. Irish author James Joyce, who once lived in Zurich, is said to have described the city's Bahnhofstrasse (main downtown street) as being so clean you could eat minestrone off it! You will find a recipe for this soup on my blog.

Some of the soups in this chapter can work as a main course, such as the Bündner Gerstensuppe (Graubünden barley soup, p. 35) from Graubünden, or the Soupe de la Mère Royaume (Mother Royaume soup, p. 59), which I make with bacon and lentils. Others, like the Kappeler Milchsuppe (milk soup, p. 47) and the creamy St. Galler Sammetsuppe (velvet soup, p. 51), are very rich, so you might prefer to serve them as a first course or side dish.

With the arrival of autumn, you will start seeing and hearing the word Suppenzeit (soup time) in the country's German-speaking regions. Of course, the desire for hot bowls of soup when the temperature starts to fall is not limited to Switzerland. Swiss soups are not just for fall and winter. For example, Soupe de Chalet (chalet soup, p. 31) from Fribourg, with macaroni and cheese, was historically made in the mountains in the summertime.

01 PÔCHOUSE DU LÉMAN

LAKE FISH SOUP

This fish soup is served in the canton of Vaud, particularly along the shores of Lac Léman (Lake Geneva). Use your favorite lake fish for this recipe, keeping in mind to adjust the cooking time, as needed, for the type of fish.

Servings: 4

Prep: 15–20 mins
Cook: 45–60 mins

INGREDIENTS:

1 tablespoon olive oil

1 tablespoon unsalted butter

1 medium onion, finely chopped (½ cup)

1 small leek, finely chopped (1 ¼ cups)

1 clove garlic, minced

1 celery stalk, finely chopped (½ cup)

1 carrot, finely chopped (½ cup)

1 tablespoon all-purpose flour

¼ teaspoon turmeric

½ teaspoon dried thyme

1 bay leaf

80 ml dry white wine (e.g., Chasselas or Sauvignon Blanc) (⅓ cup)

1 liter vegetable stock (p. 19) (4 ¼ cups)

200 g lake fish (e.g., perch or pike), skinned (7 oz)

60 ml light cream (¼ cup)

salt and freshly ground black pepper, to taste

TO GARNISH:

fresh chives, finely chopped

herbed croutons (p. 21)

INSTRUCTIONS:

1. Add the olive oil and butter to a medium saucepan over medium heat. Then add the onion, leeks and garlic. Cook for about 5 minutes or until they soften and the onions become translucent.

2. While the onions are cooking, add the chopped celery and carrot to a small bowl. Add the flour and stir until the vegetables are evenly coated. When the onions are translucent, add the celery and carrot to the saucepan along with the turmeric and cook for a few minutes, stirring frequently.

3. Stir in the white wine, scraping the bottom to remove any browned bits. Then stir in the thyme and add the bay leaf. Pour in the vegetable stock and bring the mixture to a boil. Lower the heat to medium, cover the pan and simmer for about 30 minutes or until all the vegetables are fully cooked.

4. Cut the fish into 2 cm (about 1 in) pieces. Increase the heat to medium-high and add the fish. Cook for 5–10 minutes, just until the fish is done. Stir in the cream and season with salt and pepper. Serve the soup immediately, garnished with herbed croutons and chives.

A SWISS FRENCH LAKE FISH SOUP FOR A FESTIVE SUPPER

CANTONS VAUD AND GENEVA

Lausanne à Table organizes a program of culinary events each year in Vaud's capital city, and they certainly know how to throw a party! I attended the association's 2018 launch event one sunny spring day on the shores of Lac Léman (Lake Geneva). The menu highlighted local ingredients, restaurants and producers and included a delicious pôchouse (fish soup) prepared by Chef François Grognuz and his team from the Brasserie de Montbenon. For this celebration, he prepared the soup with different types of lake fish, including *féra* (a local whitefish), *perche* (perch), *gardon* (common roach), *brochet* (pike) and *écrevisse* (crayfish). My bowl was garnished with croutons and the head of a crayfish.

Pôchouse du Léman resembles bouillabaisse, a French soup commonly made with saltwater fish, mussels and tomatoes. The Burgundy region of France also makes a pôchouse with freshwater fish. You will find the Swiss version of pôchouse particularly in Lausanne and its surrounding lakeside towns. There are a few restaurants that still serve this dish, such as the Brasserie de Montbenon. You can also find it outside of Lausanne at the Auberge

de la Gare in Grandvaux. The recipe created by the restaurant's owners, Philippe and Raymonde Delessert, serves six people and calls for 2 kilograms (almost 4 ½ lb) of fish bones to create the broth for the soup.

In a 2014 radio interview with Radio Télévision Suisse (a Swiss French broadcaster), Chef Gaël Brandy of La Pinte Vaudoise in Pully (*pinte* is a Swiss French term for a café or bistro) shared his recipe for this fish soup. He suggested that listeners could add some turmeric, which he and the host agreed would create a "pôchouse exotique." I took his advice and incorporated this into my own recipe. It not only gives the soup an additional flavor but also a lively yellow color.

For an authentic experience, I recommend you order this soup at a restaurant, but for an equally satisfying and festive supper at home, this recipe is for you!

SOUPE DE CHALET

CHALET SOUP

I like to think of this recipe as a soup version of Swiss macaroni and cheese. It was traditionally made with ingredients on hand during the summer months in the Alpine pastures and provided a hearty, nourishing meal after a long day's work. Today, people appreciate this soup year-round in many variations.

Servings: 4–6

Prep: 20–30 mins
Cook: 15–20 mins

INGREDIENTS:

1 tablespoon unsalted butter

1 medium onion, finely chopped (½ cup)

1 small leek, finely chopped (1 ¼ cups)

1 carrot, peeled and grated (½ cup)

1 medium potato, peeled and finely diced (¾ cup)

500 ml milk (2 cups)

1 liter vegetable stock (p. 19) (4 ¼ cups)

100 g small elbow macaroni (¾ cup)

60 g fresh spinach, finely chopped (about 2 handfuls)

60 ml light cream (¼ cup)

100 g Gruyère, grated (1 cup)

salt and pepper, to taste

TO GARNISH:

herbed croutons (p. 21)

INSTRUCTIONS:

1. Melt the butter in a medium saucepan over medium heat. Add the onion, leek and carrot and sauté for about 5 minutes until the onion becomes translucent. Then, add the potato and cook for a few minutes more.

2. Add the milk and vegetable stock to the saucepan and bring to a boil. Then add the macaroni and cook for 8–10 minutes, stirring occasionally, or until they are cooked.

3. Once the macaroni and potato are cooked, add the chopped spinach, cream and cheese. Stir until the spinach has wilted and the cheese has melted, and these ingredients are evenly distributed. Season the soup with salt and pepper, and garnish with herbed croutons.

Make-ahead tip:
You can cook the macaroni in advance and add it to the soup after the vegetables have fully cooked in the broth. Some people always make the soup this way, as it prevents the macaroni from becoming overcooked.

Alpine cheesemakers at supper, 1908

FRIBOURG'S MACARONI AND CHEESE SOUP

CANTON FRIBOURG

"You need to order something else. A bowl of soup won't be enough," said my mother, visiting us from the US. We were seated in the restaurant at La Maison du Gruyère, Switzerland's first demonstration cheese dairy, which opened in 1969. I tried to reassure her that I would have enough to eat.

Soupe de Chalet (chalet soup) gets its name from where it was originally made in the canton of Fribourg. During the summer months, the *armaillis* (mountain shepherds), would work in the Alpine pastures tending to their herd of cows and sleep in *chalet d'alpage* (high mountain chalets). At suppertime, they prepared simple meals with what was available, such as non-perishable dry pasta they carried with them on the hike up to the chalet. They made soup with the pasta by adding milk, cream and cheese. To give the soup some color and additional nutrients, they foraged for nettles or wild spinach (a.k.a. Good King Henry, *Chenopodium bonus-henricus*).

A friend who grew up in the district of Gruyère says that unlike in the past, when it was a simple dish for farmers, she views Soupe de Chalet today as a celebratory dish reserved for special occasions. She also says her mother gets upset when people make changes to this traditional soup! Updated recipes sometimes include ingredients such as kohlrabi and red kidney beans. My recipe is generally in keeping with tradition, but I like to add a finely chopped red bell pepper to the pot when in season during the summer months (do not tell my friends from Fribourg!). In winter, I add a carrot. These vegetables give the soup some added color and flavor to balance the richness of the milk, cheese and cream.

Back at La Maison du Gruyère, my bowl of Soupe de Chalet—filled with a steaming mix of macaroni, double cream, potatoes and Gruyère cheese—was a more than adequate main course. Whether you serve this soup for a special occasion or a weeknight supper as was historically done, no one will complain about still being hungry after the meal!

BÜNDNER GERSTENSUPPE

GRAUBÜNDEN BARLEY SOUP

03

My recipe for this soup from Graubünden calls for Bündnerfleisch, an air-dried beef, but you can easily omit this ingredient for a vegetarian version. I have also added a Spanish smoked paprika, a non-traditional ingredient, for a little more color and flavor.

Servings: 4

Prep: about 30 mins
Cook: 50–60 mins

INGREDIENTS:

1 tablespoon unsalted butter

1 medium onion, finely chopped (½ cup)

1 small leek, finely chopped (1 ¼ cups)

1 clove garlic, minced

1 carrot, finely chopped (½ cup)

150 g celery root, finely chopped (1 ½ cups)

50–60 g Bündnerfleisch, finely diced (or other thinly sliced dried beef) (about 2 oz)

½ teaspoon pimentón (Spanish smoked paprika)

1 bay leaf

125 g pearl barley (½ cup)

1 ¾ liters vegetable stock (p. 19) (7 cups)

80 ml light cream (⅓ cup)

salt and pepper, to taste

TO GARNISH:

1 handful fresh chives, finely chopped

INSTRUCTIONS:

1. Melt the butter in a medium saucepan over medium heat. When melted, add the onion, leek and garlic. Cook slowly for about 5 minutes, stirring occasionally, until the onion becomes translucent.

2. Add the carrot, celery root, dried beef, pimentón and bay leaf. Stir everything together. Cook for 2–3 minutes. Then stir in the barley and cook for another 1–2 minutes, stirring frequently.

3. Pour the vegetable stock into the saucepan. Stir everything together and bring to a boil. Then lower the heat, cover the pan and let the soup simmer for 45–60 minutes until the barley and vegetables are fully cooked.

4. Stir in the cream and season the soup with salt and pepper. Garnish with the freshly chopped chives and serve immediately.

GRAUBÜNDEN'S FAMOUS BARLEY SOUP

CANTON
GRAUBÜNDEN

For several years now, I have attended the St. Moritz Gourmet Festival. This winter event takes place within the historic palace hotels of the Engadin Valley, where winter tourism first started in Switzerland. These stunning hotels often have Bündner Gerstensuppe on their menus. One of the first things I do when I arrive at my hotel is to have a bowl of this satisfying barley soup.

If you have spent time in Graubünden, you might associate Bündner Gerstensuppe with outdoor activities, such as skiing or hiking. However, it is not just eaten in winter, and I have a fond memory of enjoying this soup on a summer hike with my family at a mountain restaurant above Pontresina. I have also had a summertime bowl of barley soup at Alphütte Fops, situated at 1,886 meters (about 6,188 feet) above sea level, while taking in the incredible views of the mountain peaks across the Lenzerheide valley.

Barley as an ingredient has existed in Alpine areas of Switzerland since the Bronze Age. It grows well in areas with harsher climates and lower soil quality. High in fiber, the barley used for today's Gerstensuppe has been pearled—both the outer husk and the bran layers have been removed. It has a lighter color than hulled barley, which only has the outer husk removed.

Graubünden is not the only Swiss canton with a barley soup. The Appenzell region has Gsöödsoppe. Like the Bündner version, it contains chopped vegetables and cream, but the Appenzeller soup traditionally includes beans such as navy or borlotti beans. A 1907 cookbook published in Chur, Graubünden's capital city, has a recipe for Gerstensuppe that also includes dried beans, and some modern recipes often do as well.

A common ingredient in today's Gerstensuppe is Bündnerfleisch, an air-dried raw-cured beef, also from Graubünden. Some recipes call for adding a Kalbsfüsschen (calf's foot), bacon or other smoked pork. To give it a smoky flavor, I have opted for the addition of pimentón, a Spanish paprika.

Whether you dine on this soup in a mountain hut, a five-star hotel or at home, it will taste just as good.

BASLER MEHLSUPPE

BASEL FLOUR SOUP

I have updated Basel's traditional flour soup by adding a handful of brown lentils and chopped carrots. They enhance the smoky flavor of the broth created by toasting the flour.

Servings: 4–6

Prep: about 30 mins
Cook: 45–60 mins

INGREDIENTS:

60 g all-purpose flour (½ cup)

1 tablespoon unsalted butter

1 large onion, chopped (1 cup)

1 large carrot, chopped (1 cup)

1 clove garlic, minced

120 ml red wine (½ cup)

50 g brown lentils (¼ cup)

1 bay leaf

1 sprig fresh thyme
(or ¼ teaspoon dried thyme)

1 liter vegetable stock (p. 19)
(4 ¼ cups)

salt and pepper, to taste

TO GARNISH:

Gruyère, Sbrinz or Parmesan, grated

SERVING SUGGESTION:

Fastenwähe (recipe in my *Swiss Bread* book, p. 171)

INSTRUCTIONS:

1. Heat the flour in a medium frying pan over medium heat. Stir the flour frequently with a whisk for 15–20 minutes until it turns a light chestnut brown, like the color of cinnamon — you will need to watch it very carefully or it will burn! Pour the flour onto a plate to cool.

2. In a medium saucepan, add the butter, onion, carrot and garlic. Cook over medium heat until the onion becomes translucent. Whisk in the red wine and flour until well combined. Then stir in the lentils, bay leaf and thyme.

3. Pour in the vegetable stock. Stir everything together and bring to a boil. Reduce the heat, cover the pan and let it simmer for 45–60 minutes, stirring occasionally. The lentils and carrots should be soft and tender.

4. Remove the bay leaf and sprig of thyme from the soup. Puree the soup with an upright or immersion blender until smooth. Serve immediately with a generous sprinkle of grated cheese.

BASEL'S BROWNED FLOUR SOUP

CANTON BASEL-STADT

When my son came home from school one day and discovered we were having Basler Mehlsuppe (flour soup) for lunch, he groaned. His teacher had somehow convinced him that this soup tasted awful. Honestly, I had my doubts as well.

The local legend in Basel attributes the creation of its flour soup to a woman in love. According to the Museum der Kulturen Basel (Basel Museum of Cultures), she was cooking and chatting casually about her romance with her servants when she realized the flour in her pan was turning brown. Instead of throwing it out, she turned it into a delicious soup. Another legend in Basel says that women used to not be eligible for marriage until it was proven they could make a good flour soup.

Once considered an austere dish for Lent, people especially ate it during the time between Ash Wednesday and Easter. Since 1835, however, this soup has remained one of the most important culinary offerings at Fasnacht, Basel's carnival celebration. In local dialect, the Basler Fasnacht is referred to as the *drey scheenschte Dääg* (three most beautiful days). The event kicks off

on the first Monday after Ash Wednesday, beginning with the Morgenstraich (early morning parade). Along with a slice of Basel's famous onion tart, cheese tart and a Fastenwähe, a little bread with four holes that is sprinkled with caraway seeds, flour soup is a must!

Mehlsuppe is not only limited to Basel. I also came across a few recipes in the canton of Neuchâtel for a similar soup known as Soupe de pompiers (firefighters' soup). Described as a cross between an onion soup and a flour soup, it supposedly earned its name from being served by local restaurants to thank firefighters after they had put out a fire in the community.

That day at home when I first made this soup, my son and I were pleasantly surprised by its smoky flavor. Years later, I developed my own version of this simple recipe to make it a bit more robust for a weeknight supper and it has become a staple dish in my family.

⬤ 05 BÜRBORA

PUMPKIN SOUP

I make this delicious pumpkin soup from Ticino with butternut squash. Adding a handful of short–grained rice to the pureed soup makes this a filling dish for supper.

Servings: 4

Prep: 15–20 mins
Cook: about 1 hour

INGREDIENTS:

1 tablespoon unsalted butter

1 medium onion, chopped (½ cup)

1 small leek, chopped (1 ¼ cups)

500 g butternut squash (or other squash), cut into 3 cm (1 in) pieces (2 cups)

750 ml vegetable stock (p. 19) (3 cups)

100 g risotto rice (e.g., Arborio or Loto) (½ cup)

1 pinch nutmeg

250 ml milk (1 cup)

salt and pepper, to taste

SUGGESTED TOPPINGS:

crème fraiche or pumpkin seed oil

crispy lardons or crumbled bacon

fresh parsley, finely chopped

INSTRUCTIONS:

1. In a medium saucepan, melt the butter over medium heat. Add the onion and leek to the pan. Cook for about 5 minutes, stirring frequently, until the onions become translucent.

2. Add the squash and vegetable stock. Bring to a boil and reduce the heat. Cover the pan and let it simmer for 15–20 minutes. When the squash has softened, blend the soup until smooth with an immersion or upright blender.

3. Return the soup to the stove on medium heat and stir in the rice and nutmeg. Cover the pan and let the mixture simmer for 20–30 minutes until the rice is fully cooked. Then take the pan off the heat and stir in the milk. Season with salt and pepper.

4. Serve immediately and garnish with the suggested toppings.

TICINO'S BURBLING PUMPKIN SOUP

CANTON TICINO

Held around mid–September, the nationwide Settimana del Gusto (Week of Taste) highlights regional food products and promotes sustainable culinary practices with environmental and health benefits, particularly for younger generations. The canton of Ticino has organized a special menu for schools during this week for several years now. The menu features typical Ticinese dishes, such as a pumpkin soup called Bürbora. When I first heard about it, I was curious about how it got its name!

According to Mark Bertogliati, curator of the Museo etnografico della Valle di Muggio (Ethnographic Museum of the Muggio Valley), Bürbora is known throughout Ticino, but originally comes from Lugano and its neighboring valleys. He writes, "the expressive term 'bürbora' is probably of onomatopoeic origin. For example, 'bul-,' or 'bur-' could be considered as mimicking the burbling sound of the soup when it boils." In the Mendrisiotto district, "similar terms (*balburena, barburina, barbureta*) actually indicate a soup prepared with maize [corn]

flour." He mentioned that people would add pumpkin and a handful of rice for variety, as well as a glass or two of wine when taking the soup off the heat.

A 1980 video shared by Radiotelevisione svizzera (a Swiss Italian broadcaster) on Facebook shows Agnese Weber from Meride, a village in the Mendrisiotto district, explaining how to make Bürbora. Her recipe, which includes flour, rice and milk, came from her mother. She says it reminds her of fall with the arrival of cooler temperatures and the harvest of chestnuts and hazelnuts.

For my recipe, I have added some short-grained rice but no flour because I do not want to further dilute the flavor of the squash. I like to use this soup as a canvas for multiple savory toppings, such as bacon, crème fraiche or pumpkin seed oil, that complement the sweetness of the pumpkin or squash. Whether you serve your wine in the soup or on the side, this is a fortifying Ticinese dish to usher in the fall.

KAPPELER MILCHSUPPE
KAPPEL MILK SOUP

This soup supposedly stopped a war, at least temporarily, when the two sides shared a simple meal of bread and milk. This is another great recipe for using up your stale bread. A bowl of this soup is quite filling, so I recommend serving it in a cup instead.

Servings: 4–6

Prep: 35 mins (includes 30 mins resting time)
Cook: about 15 mins

INGREDIENTS:

1 liter whole milk (4 ¼ cups)

1 small handful fresh basil leaves

10 peppercorns

1 pinch piment d'Espelette or cayenne pepper

1 medium onion, chopped (½ cup)

1 clove garlic, minced

1 tablespoon unsalted butter

2 tablespoons all-purpose flour

½ teaspoon salt

freshly ground black pepper, to taste

TO GARNISH:

1–2 tablespoons unsalted butter

4–5 slices of bread, cubed for croutons

Sbrinz or Gruyère, grated

fresh parsley

INSTRUCTIONS:

1. Add the milk, basil, peppercorns and piment d'Espelette to a medium saucepan and bring to a boil. Then take the pan off the heat, cover it and let it sit for 30 minutes.

2. Pour the seasoned milk through a sieve into a bowl. Set the milk aside.

3. Mix the onions and garlic with the flour in a bowl until they are well combined. Melt the butter in a medium saucepan over medium heat and then add the onion and garlic mixture. Cook the onions for about 5 minutes, until they become translucent. Then, gently pour in the seasoned milk and add the salt. Blend until smooth using an upright or immersion blender.

4. Return the soup to the stove on medium heat. Season with freshly ground black pepper. Cook for a few minutes more until heated through. Keep the soup at a low simmer while you prepare the garnish.

5. Melt the butter in a medium frying pan to make the croutons. Add the cubed bread and toast until lightly browned, flipping the pieces to make sure both sides get some color. Serve the soup garnished with the croutons, grated cheese and parsley.

SWITZERLAND'S WAR-STOPPING SOUP

CANTONS ZURICH AND ZUG

On my 44th birthday, I had two objectives: First, buy actress Sophia Loren's favorite Swiss cake, the Baaren Räbentorte. Second, eat it while picnicking at the site of the Kappeler Milchsuppe monument.

After we stopped at the Nussbaumer bakery in Baar for this one-of-a-kind cake decorated with a turnip leaf made of marzipan, we walked up the hillside to the Milchsuppenstein (milk soup stone). The monument serves to remind visitors that a simple soup of milk and bread supposedly stopped a war, at least temporarily. This Swiss story is an example of culinary diplomacy, using food as a starting point to bridge differences.

The monument at the Milchsuppenstein in Kappel am Albis has "1529" carved into it. This was the date of the First Kappel War, a conflict between Protestants from Zurich and Catholics from Lucerne, Uri, Schwyz, Unterwalden, and Zug during the Swiss Reformation. Situated on the border between the cantons of Zurich and Zug, the monument marks the spot where soldiers from the two sides came together. While their leaders negotiated a peace treaty,

these hungry soldiers supposedly shared ingredients to make a soup of milk and bread. Unfortunately, the deal fell apart two years later, leading to the Second Kappel War. Another monument in the same town honors Huldrych Zwingli, the Protestant leader killed in this ongoing conflict.

Over the years, the Kappeler Milchsuppe has been depicted in artworks and has reappeared at modern Swiss events as a symbol of cooperation and compromise. Martin Dahinden, Switzerland's former Ambassador to the US writes in his book *Beyond Muesli and Fondue* that when you make this soup, "traditionally, everyone eats out of the same soup tureen." Many recipes exist for this legendary soup, with countless variations, as no one knows what really happened on that bucolic hillside hundreds of years ago. Today, the Milchsuppenstein is a lovely place to picnic with a delicious slice of Räbentorte and a reminder that food is still an important way to bring people together.

ST. GALLER SAMMETSUPPE

ST. GALLEN VELVET SOUP

This quick recipe calls for simple ingredients that you likely already have on hand. I add homemade baked potato slices as a garnish to complement the soup's velvety texture. The key to achieving this smooth consistency is rapid whisking!

Servings: 2 bowls or 4 cups

Prep: about 10 mins
Cook: 10–15 mins

INGREDIENTS:

2 tablespoons unsalted butter

500 ml vegetable stock (p. 19)
(2 cups)

30 g all-purpose flour (¼ cup)

60 ml milk (¼ cup)

60 ml light cream (¼ cup)

1 egg yolk

salt and pepper, to taste

TO GARNISH:

baked potato slices (p. 52)

Mostbröckli or dried beef, finely
diced (optional)

fresh chives, finely chopped

INSTRUCTIONS:

1. In a medium saucepan over medium heat, melt the butter. While the butter is melting, heat the vegetable stock in a small saucepan until it simmers.

2. Sift the flour over the melted butter in the pan, then whisk it together to create a smooth paste. Take the pan off the heat and slowly whisk in the heated vegetable stock until it has fully absorbed the paste. Return the pan to the stove over medium-high heat and bring the soup to a boil.

3. In a bowl, whisk together the milk, cream and egg yolk until fully combined. Pour it into the boiling broth in a thin ribbon, while constantly whisking the broth to prevent the egg from curdling. Continue whisking until fully heated and the mixture comes to a low boil. Season with salt and pepper. Garnish with baked potato slices, Mostbröckli (optional) and chives.

BAKED POTATO SLICES

Servings: 1–2 handfuls

Prep: 5–10 mins
Bake: about 10–15 mins

INGREDIENTS:

1–2 large baking potatoes

1–2 tablespoons canola or rapeseed oil

salt, to taste

INSTRUCTIONS:

1. Slice the potatoes thinly (e.g., with a mandolin). Add the slices to a bowl with the oil and mix with your hands to make sure the slices are well coated.

2. Place the potato slices on a baking tray lined with parchment paper. Bake at 200°C (400°F) for 10–15 minutes until they become fully cooked, slightly crisp and lightly browned, gently flipping them halfway through. Keep an eye on them, so they do not burn. Sprinkle them with salt before serving.

A GOLDEN, VELVETY SOUP FROM ST. GALLEN

CANTON ST. GALLEN

In 2018, following the announcement of the election results for Switzerland's Federal Council, an apéro was served under the dome of the Bundeshaus (parliament building). Elected officials feasted on regional dishes from around the country, including a simple soup from the canton of St. Gallen known as Sammetsuppe. In German, its name means "velvet soup." The velvety consistency comes from the egg yolk and cream beaten into the broth just before it is served.

These days it can be hard to find Sammetsuppe at a restaurant in St. Gallen. One restaurant that still serves it is Zum Bäumli, an example of the city's historic Erststockbeizli (first–floor taverns). In the old city center, where buildings were constructed on wooden piles over the soft, wet ground, restaurants avoided serving guests on the damp and often dimly lit ground floor, opting instead for the sunnier first floor. At Zum Bäumli, they refer to their velvet soup as "Appenzeller Sammetsuppe." The neighboring cantons of Appenzell Ausserrhoden and Appenzell Innerrhoden put their own spin on this recipe by adding

Mostbröckli. The oldest mention of this smoked, dried beef from the region dates to 1905. It earned an *indication géographique protégée* (protected geographic indication) designation in 2018. Mostbröckli bearing this label must be produced in Appenzell or in certain parts of St. Gallen. Always sliced thinly, this dried meat adds some color and a smoky flavor to this mild soup.

For a vegetarian version, or if you cannot get your hands on Mostbröckli to garnish the soup, you can use my recipe for baked potato slices. Gently place a few of these slices on top of this creamy soup, sprinkle on some fresh chives and you have an easy supper—good enough to celebrate your own personal victories at home.

08 SOLEDURNER WYSÜPPLI

SOLOTHURN WINE SOUP

This recipe works well for a Friday or Saturday night supper, served with some crusty bread and a salad. Or present it as a starter before a celebratory meal. This French-influenced soup has enough wine that you should not serve it to children, at least not in large quantities!

Servings: 4–6

Prep: 20–30 mins
Cook: about 1 ½ hrs

INGREDIENTS:

2 tablespoons unsalted butter

1 medium onion, finely chopped (½ cup)

1 small leek, finely chopped (1¼ cups)

1 carrot, grated (¾ cup)

1 celery stalk, finely chopped (½ cup)

1 tablespoon all-purpose flour

1 sprig fresh thyme (or 1 pinch of dried thyme)

1 bay leaf

400 ml dry white wine (e.g., Chasselas or Sauvignon Blanc) (1 ⅔ cups)

600 ml vegetable stock (p. 19) (2 ½ cups)

60 ml light cream (¼ cup)

salt and pepper, to taste

TO GARNISH:

1 tablespoon unsalted butter

75 g mushrooms, sliced (1 cup)

salt and pepper, to taste

fresh parsley, finely chopped

sprinkle of piment d'Espelette (optional)

INSTRUCTIONS:

1. In a medium saucepan, melt the butter over medium heat. Add the onion and leek to the pan and sauté for about 5 minutes until they soften and the onion becomes translucent.

2. Add the carrot and celery to a bowl and toss with the flour until well combined. Then add this mixture to the saucepan and continue cooking for another 5–7 minutes, stirring frequently.

3. Add the thyme and bay leaf and stir in the wine and vegetable stock. Increase the heat to high and bring to a boil. Then reduce the heat to medium, cover the pan and simmer for 45–60 minutes.

4. When the vegetables are tender, prepare the garnish. Melt the butter in a small frying pan over medium heat. Add the mushrooms and sauté for about 5 minutes until they soften. Season with salt and pepper.

5. Stir the light cream into the soup and season with salt and pepper. Add the soup to bowls. Garnish with the sauteed mushrooms and parsley, and sprinkle with piment d'Espelette (optional).

SOLOTHURN'S
FRENCH-INFLUENCED WINE SOUP

CANTON SOLOTHURN

Traveling to Solothurn by boat is not an obvious way to reach this landlocked cantonal capital, but an Aare River cruise from the bilingual city of Biel (German) / Bienne (French) will get you there. During just such a cruise, I first tried one of Solothurn's most well-known dishes, the Soledurner Wysüppli.

The part of the Aare River that I traveled on to reach Solothurn was previously used to transport barrels of wine. The story goes that workers on these boats could drink all the wine they wanted during the trip, which led to a local expression still used today, "être sur Soleure." It literally means "to be in Solothurn," but figuratively, it signifies someone who has had too much to drink. Knowing this, it might seem appropriate for a wine soup to be a Solothurner specialty!

According to the Bürgergemeinde Solothurn, the municipal organization for this community, the birth of the Soledurner Wysüppli likely has a French connection. From the 16th to 18th centuries, a French ambassador appointed by the King of France took up residence in the city, in

part to oversee the management of Swiss mercenaries. The city's wine soup is said to have been created during this period.

The Bürgergemeinde Solothurn also maintains the Domaine de Soleure, a community-owned vineyard that uses the French name for the city. The Domaine's recipe for the Soledurner Wysüppli recommends some variations, such as adding snails for a Fasnächtliches Wysüppli (carnival soup). For festive occasions, they suggest adding veal sweetbreads and mushrooms.

I decided to only include the mushrooms in my recipe, keeping it vegetarian. The quantity of wine is not insignificant and it gives a pleasantly acidic taste to the soup. If you ever get the chance, visit the Domaine and pick up a bottle of Chasselas wine for a truly authentic Wysüppli. There are also a dozen or so restaurants in the greater Solothurn area that use the Domaine's wine in their own version of the soup.

SOUPE DE LA MÈRE ROYAUME

MOTHER ROYAUME'S SOUP

My interpretation of this 17th century soup from the canton of Geneva contains lentils or rice and has crisp croutons sprinkled on top. Feel free to substitute with any winter vegetables you have on hand, such as parsnips, kale or squash. Some people say this soup tastes even better reheated the next day.

Servings: 4

Prep: 20–30 mins
Cook: 45–60 mins

INGREDIENTS:

50 g bacon, chopped (4 strips)

1 large onion, finely chopped
(1 cup)

1 small leek, halved, thinly sliced
(1 ¼ cups)

1 small turnip, finely chopped
(1 cup)

1 large carrot, grated (1 cup)

1 large handful cabbage, thinly
sliced (1 cup)

50 g brown lentils (or rice)
(¼ cup)

2 liters vegetable stock (p. 19)
(8 ½ cups)

1 small handful fresh chervil
or parsley, finely chopped

salt and freshly ground black
pepper, to taste

TO GARNISH:

herbed croutons (p. 21)

SERVING SUGGESTION:

Sweet Potato Weggli (as
shown in the photo). Recipe via
cuisinehelvetica.com

INSTRUCTIONS:

1. Cook the bacon in a medium saucepan over medium heat until it browns and becomes crispy.

2. Add the onions and leek. Stir everything together and cook for about 5 minutes until the leek softens and the onion becomes translucent.

3. Add the turnip, carrot and cabbage to the pan. Sauté for a few minutes over medium heat, stirring frequently.

4. Finally, add the lentils, vegetable broth and herbs. Bring the soup to a boil. Then reduce the heat, cover the pan and simmer for about 30 minutes until the lentils are fully cooked. Season with salt and pepper, as needed. Serve immediately with some herbed croutons sprinkled on top.

A LEGENDARY SOUP
THAT STOPPED THE SAVOYARDS

CANTON GENEVE

Soupe de la Mère Royaume has a connection to Geneva's Fête de l'Escalade. During this annual celebration, the community commemorates the successful thwarting of the Duke of Savoy's attempt to gain control over the city. In December 1602, the Duke directed more than 2,000 of his troops to scale the city walls and claim it for the Savoyards.

That fateful night, when the soldiers arrived and the church bells sounded the alarm, the citizens of Geneva took it upon themselves to stop the invasion. Legend has it that a woman named Catherine Royaume, known today as Mère Royaume (Mother Royaume), threw her soup cauldron and its scalding contents out the window onto the enemy to prevent them from advancing. This tenacious act epitomizes the determination of the *Genevois* to do everything they could to protect their city. And they succeeded!

Today, you will find many different versions of this famous soup. For my recipe, I have included seasonal vegetables that would have been used in this region during

the 17th century, according to research conducted by the Alimentarium, the world's first-ever food-themed museum in Vevey. They include cabbage, onion, turnip and leek. My recipe also calls for lentils, another typical soup ingredient from that time.

To celebrate Mère Royaume, chocolatiers in Geneva also make *marmites* (chocolate cauldrons) filled with sweet little marzipan versions of her vegetables. Decorated with the city's colors—red and yellow—the cauldron also features its coat of arms. Around December 12, the *Genevois* have a ritual that accompanies eating the *marmite*. Two people join hands and recite the words, "ainsi périrent (or périssent) les ennemis de la République." This translates to something like, "thus perished (or perishes) the enemies of the Republic!" Then, they smash the chocolate cauldron with their clasped fists. Smashing chocolate and then getting to eat it? It's one of my favorite Swiss traditions.

POTATOES

Potatoes did not arrive in Europe until the 16th century, when Spaniards brought them from South America. It was actually a Swiss Botanist called Gaspard Bauhin who in 1596 gave potatoes their scientific name, *Solanum tuberosum esculentum* (changed later to just *Solanum tuberosum*). Many people, including Bauhin, once thought these strange new tubers from the New World caused leprosy! Some say it was because the gnarled appearance of the potatoes reminded them of someone suffering from this disease. At one point, growing potatoes was even banned in the Franche-Comté region of France, which borders Switzerland.

Today, potatoes of all varieties are an indispensable ingredient in Swiss cuisine. It would be hard to imagine Switzerland without Rösti (p. 81) or the beloved Papet Vaudois, a sausage dish from Vaud served with leeks and potatoes (you will find a recipe on my blog). The versatile potato can be used throughout the year and the country consumes about 45 kilograms per person annually. This figure incorporates potatoes in all forms, including potato chips. While this chapter is devoted to potatoes, you will find them as an ingredient in at least one recipe in every chapter of this book, except for the sweet recipes in Chapter VIII.

This chapter covers all the ways the Swiss like to prepare their potatoes—mashed, boiled, fried and baked. Two recipes, Rösti and Kartoffelsalat (potato salad, p. 73), can be found throughout the country, while the other recipes have more regional ties. There are two from French-speaking Switzerland: a tomato fondue from Valais with boiled potatoes (p. 69) and a potato quenelles dish from the Jura (p. 65). One of my favorite recipes in this chapter, Stupfete (p. 93), is also one of the easiest to make in the entire book. I give you advice on the type of potato to choose for each dish.

10 FLOUTES

POTATO QUENELLES

An elegant way to serve mashed potatoes, Floutes are found in the canton of Jura. You will need two big spoons to form the special elongated egg-like shape, known as a "quenelle." Serve as a main course with a salad or as a side dish.

Servings: 4

INGREDIENTS:

1 kg potatoes (e.g., Yukon Gold or Bintje) (2 ¼ lb)

3 ½ teaspoons salt

3 tablespoons all-purpose flour

3 tablespoons unsalted butter

80 ml light cream (⅓ cup)

50 g Gruyère (or other cheese), grated (½ cup)

TO GARNISH:

freshly ground black pepper

green onions, finely chopped or crispy onions (p. 99)

fresh parsley, finely chopped

TIP:

You can also use leftover mashed potatoes to make this dish. Omit the salt in step 2 if they already contain salt. If your potatoes have been in the refrigerator, you may need to increase the baking time

Prep: 45-60 mins (inc. boiling the potatoes)
Bake: 20–25 mins

INSTRUCTIONS:

1. Add the whole, unpeeled potatoes to a medium–sized pot with 2 teaspoons of salt. Add enough cold water to just cover them. Bring the water to a boil, lower the temperature to medium-high and cook the potatoes until tender (about 30–45 minutes).

2. When the potatoes are done, take them off the heat and drain the water. Let them cool until they are safe to touch and then peel. Pass the potatoes through a food mill or ricer into a large bowl or use a potato masher. Mix the flour and 1 ½ teaspoons salt into the mashed potatoes until well combined.

3. Grease a 28 cm (11 in) round or 23 x 33 cm (9 x 13 in) rectangular oven-safe gratin dish.

4. Melt the butter. Dip two large soup spoons in the butter and use them to make quenelles with the potato mixture. Do this by taking a large scoop of the potato mixture in one spoon and passing the mixture back and forth between the spoons, turning and smoothing each side until you have an elongated egg shape. Place the quenelles directly into the prepared ceramic dish in a single layer. Continue this process until the pan is filled.

5. Pour the cream over the potato quenelles and sprinkle with the grated cheese. Bake for about 20–25 minutes at 200°C (400°F) until the cheese has melted and the edges of the quenelles have started to brown. Take the pan out of the oven and sprinkle with black pepper. Top with the green onions and the parsley and serve immediately.

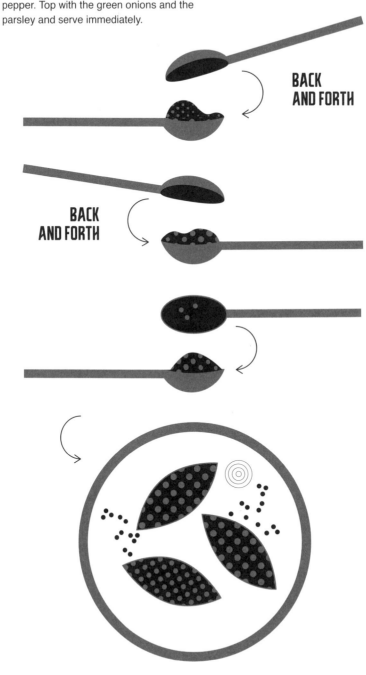

BACK
AND FORTH

BACK
AND FORTH

AN ELEGANT WAY TO USE UP LEFTOVER MASHED POTATOES

CANTON JURA

I first learned how to shape quenelles from Claude Frôté, the former chef of the Michelin-starred Bocca restaurant in St. Blaise. It was during a cooking class that he was teaching at Les Laboratoires Culinaires in Neuchâtel, where I live. Years later, I watched him make quenelles again for Floutes Jurassiennes on one of my favorite Swiss cooking programs, *Pique Assiette* with Annick Jeanmairet.

As indicated by the name of this dish, Floutes Jurassiennes are found in the canton of Jura. My friend who grew up near Porrentruy describes them as "the Jura-version of gnocchi." They are a great way to cut down on food waste—leftover potatoes can be formed into a new shape and revived with some butter, cream and cheese. Across the border from Switzerland in the Alsace region of France, the dish is known as *pfloutes*, and in German-speaking Switzerland, as *Kartoffelpfluten*.

A common way to make Floutes is to dip the potato quenelles in melted butter before adding them to the baking dish. While I have tried that method, I prefer the technique described in the 1960s by cookbook author Elisabeth Fülscher. Instead of dipping the quenelles in butter after you make them, you dip the spoons in the butter before you make them, to help smooth out the mashed potatoes.

There are many possible ways to change up your Floutes. Different ingredients can be added to the potatoes, such as garlic, herbs and cheese, or you can vary the toppings by using bacon, mushrooms, steamed broccoli or crispy onions (p. 99).

I really enjoy shaping the potato quenelles for this dish and trying to make them look perfect. You will find a how-to video for this recipe on my blog. Thanks again to Claude Frôté for teaching me this technique!

FONDUE À LA TOMATE

TOMATO FONDUE WITH BOILED POTATOES

Fresh tomatoes give this cheese fondue a pleasing kick of acidity. They also give it a lightness in comparison to a traditional cheese fondue, making it a nice option for warmer months. You typically serve this fondue with boiled potatoes, but I also like it with cubed bread.

Servings: 4

Prep: about 45 mins (incl. boiling the potatoes)
Cook: 20–30 mins

INGREDIENTS:

1 clove garlic, peeled and halved

175 ml dry white wine (e.g., Fendant* or Sauvignon Blanc) (¾ cup)

1 tablespoon cornstarch

300 g Gruyère, grated (10 oz)

300 g Raclette, finely diced (10 oz)

2 medium tomatoes, seeded and finely chopped, room temperature (1 ½ cups)

SERVE WITH:

potatoes, boiled in their skins (e.g., new potatoes, Yukon Gold or Charlotte) cubed bread (e.g., Glarnerbrot, p. 221)

*In Valais, wine made with the Chasselas variety of grapes is called Fendant.

INSTRUCTIONS:

1. In a small bowl, whisk together the white wine and the cornstarch until well combined. In another bowl, toss the two grated cheeses together until evenly distributed.

2. Rub the cut surface of the halved garlic on the inside of a fondue pot. Stir about 50 ml (scant ¼ cup) of the wine mixture into the fondue pot. Put the pot on the stove over medium heat. When the wine starts to simmer, add about one-quarter of the cheese. Stir the mixture frequently in a figure-eight motion for about 5 minutes until the cheese has melted. Then add half of the remaining cheese and wine mixtures to the fondue. Continue stirring until all the cheese has melted, about 8–10 minutes. After that, stir in the tomatoes with the remaining cheese and wine mixtures.

3. When all the cheese has melted and the fondue has a smooth texture, put the fondue pot on the burner at the table. To serve, use a ladle to add spoonfuls of the melted cheese onto your plate of potatoes.

A "LIGHTER" CHEESE FONDUE WITH FRESH TOMATOES

CANTON VALAIS

One day when cookbook authors Arnaud and Jennifer Favre were at a book signing in Neuchâtel, I stopped by to see them with a burning fondue question. Their popular cookbooks about fondue and raclette are published by Helvetiq, the same publisher as my cookbooks.

When it comes to cheese fondue, I am a purist. After all, this is the closest thing Switzerland has to a national dish! I prefer not to add anything extraneous that might diminish the taste of the cheese. Arnaud and Jennifer, on the other hand, have no qualms about pairing different flavors and textures with fondue. Their book contains innovative fondue recipes with ingredients such as mustard, honey and walnuts or curry with pineapple.

My question for the Favres was about a tomato fondue, which you normally serve with potatoes rather than cubed bread. Some recipes add tomato sauce to the fondue, which makes it look like a cheesy sauce for pasta. When I asked the Swiss fondue experts, they told me they use fresh tomatoes. In terms of cheese, the tomato

fondue in Valais typically uses Gruyère—as is in the traditional *moitié-moitié* (half and half) fondue—but it replaces the Vacherin Fribourgeois with Raclette.

The word fondue (past tense of the French verb fondre) means "melted." This dish has its roots in French-speaking Switzerland, but it really only became popular throughout the country following World War II, due in large part to a marketing campaign from the Schweizerische Käseunion (Swiss Cheese Union). One of its most memorable advertising slogans from the 1950s used the acronym FIGUGEGL—*"Fondue isch guet und git e gueti Luune"* (fondue is good and puts you in a good mood).

Some Swiss people feel strongly that cheese fondue has a season—and it is not summer! In my opinion, fondue can be eaten any time of year, especially in the mountains after a day of hiking. I have memories of savoring a cheese fondue one July evening while watching a World Cup soccer match at the Cabane des Violettes, a mountain hut above Crans-Montana. And when you throw some fresh tomatoes in your fondue, the acidity helps cut the richness of the cheese, making it seem a bit lighter.

KARTOFFELSALAT

POTATO SALAD

This potato salad works as a vegetarian main when served with hard-boiled eggs, for example, or as a side dish, especially during warm weather. Make sure you use a waxy potato variety that stays firm after boiling. Also, do not overcook your potatoes or they will fall apart when you mix the salad.

Servings: 4–6

Prep: 15–20 mins
Cook: 30–45 mins

INGREDIENTS:

1 kg potatoes (e.g., Annabelle, Charlotte or red-skinned potatoes) (2 ¼ lb)

2 teaspoons salt (for boiling the potatoes)

1 large bunch of radishes, thinly sliced

½ red onion, halved and sliced thinly in rings

2 tablespoons capers

1 handful parsley, finely chopped

DRESSING:

120 ml vegetable stock (p. 19) (½ cup)

2 tablespoons apple cider vinegar

1 tablespoon canola or rapeseed oil

2 teaspoons Dijon mustard

1 teaspoon salt

1 pinch cayenne pepper (optional)

freshly ground black pepper, to taste

SERVE WITH:

fresh parsley or chives, finely chopped

INSTRUCTIONS:

1. Add the potatoes to a medium saucepan, cover them with water, add the salt and bring to a boil. When the potatoes are fork tender, place them in a colander to drain and let them cool.

2. Bring the vegetable stock to a boil in the same medium saucepan and then stir in the oil, vinegar, mustard, salt and cayenne pepper. Transfer the dressing to a large heat-proof bowl.

3. Peel and slice the cooled potatoes, adding them immediately to the warm dressing to soak up the flavor. When all the potatoes are in the bowl, add the radishes, onion, capers, parsley and salt. Gently stir the potato salad together until all the ingredients are evenly distributed. Season with freshly ground black pepper.

4. Garnish the potato salad with finely chopped parsley or chives. Serve while still warm or at room temperature, or refrigerate the salad and serve chilled as part of a mixed salad.

Make-ahead tip:
Make this salad in advance and refrigerate it for no more than 2–3 days.

A SWISS POTATO SALAD
FOR WARM SUMMER EVENINGS

THROUGHOUT SWITZERLAND

"Does it have mayonnaise?" A voice from the living room inquired suspiciously. "No, don't worry," I replied. My husband refuses to eat mayonnaise. It was my first time making a Swiss Kartoffelsalat (potato salad) for supper.

I grew up eating potato salad in the US with a dressing that had mayonnaise (actually, it was Miracle Whip) and yellow mustard as its base. Along with boiled potatoes, there were onions and hard-boiled eggs but not much more. We would sometimes have it with hot dogs or hamburgers, eaten outside at a picnic table. Just thinking about it transports me back to my childhood home in the summertime.

In Switzerland, you will often see Kartoffelsalat served on its own or as part of a Swiss "mixed salad," which has several different vegetable salads served on the same plate. The beauty of a potato salad is that you can make it ahead of time. Plus, the ingredients are inexpensive and it fills you up.

When I asked some friends who grew up in Bern about Kartoffelsalat, they told me that Swiss potato salads generally fall into two categories, either the dressing is made with bouillon or with mayonnaise. I had never heard of making potato salad with bouillon before. My only experience growing up with a non–mayonnaise version was my aunt's "German Potato Salad." Served warm, it contained salty bacon, sugar and vinegar, giving it an appealing sweet and sour flavor.

For my recipe, I have chosen a dressing using vegetable stock or bouillon. The warm potatoes freshly peeled and steeped in the stock soak up the flavor. With a splash of vinegar, it reminds me a bit of my aunt's potato salad. I like it best served warm, with some hard-boiled eggs on the side.

My husband approves of this potato salad. And for the record, I love mayonnaise, especially the creamy Swiss version from a tube—just not in my potato salad!

SCHWYZER OFETURLI

SCHWYZ POTATO CAKE WITH BACON, CHEESE & MUSHROOMS

In this recipe, boiled potatoes are grated, mixed with some flour and topped with mushrooms, bacon and cheese. You will find different interpretations of Ofeturli in central Switzerland. My version is inspired by the one I tasted in Stoos.

Servings: 4–6

Prep: 30–45 mins (incl. boiling the potatoes)
Bake: 30–35 mins

INGREDIENTS:

1 kg potatoes (e.g., Yukon Gold or Bintje) (2 ¼ lb)

2 teaspoons salt (for boiling the potatoes)

75 g all-purpose flour (⅔ cup)

1 tablespoon olive oil

1 teaspoon salt

freshly ground black pepper, to taste

50 g bacon, chopped (optional) (about 4 slices)

250 g mushrooms, halved and sliced (3 ¼ cups)

100 g Sbrinz (or Parmesan), finely grated (1 cup)

200 g cheese (e.g., Gruyère or Emmentaler), grated (2 cups)

1 small onion, cut into thin rings

TO GARNISH:

fresh parsley or chives, chopped

INSTRUCTIONS:

1. Boil the unpeeled potatoes in salted water. When the potatoes have cooled, grate them into a large bowl.

2. Grease a 23 x 33 cm (9 x 13 in) rectangular oven-safe baking dish. Set aside.

3. Add the flour, olive oil, salt and pepper to the large bowl with the grated potatoes. Mix everything together until well combined. Press this mixture into the baking dish.

4. In a medium frying pan over medium-high heat, cook the bacon for several minutes until it becomes browned. Drain some of the bacon fat from the pan. Add the sliced mushrooms, reducing the heat to medium. Cook the mushrooms for about 5 minutes until they soften and become golden brown.

5. Spread the bacon and mushrooms over the mashed potato mixture in the baking dish. Then add the grated cheese in an even layer, followed by the onion slices. Cover the pan with aluminum foil and bake for 20 minutes at 180°C (350°F). Then remove the aluminum foil and bake for another 10–15 minutes until the cheese has fully melted and the potatoes are hot. Sprinkle with chopped parsley or chives and serve immediately.

Make-ahead tip:
Prepare the boiled potatoes 1–2 days in advance and keep them in the refrigerator until you are ready to use them.

You can also grate the cheese and cut the mushrooms in the morning and keep these ingredients refrigerated until you are ready to use them in the evening.

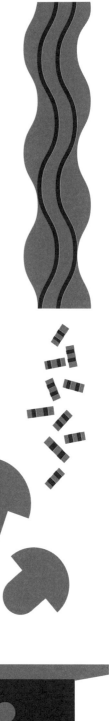

A SAVORY POTATO CAKE FROM CENTRAL SWITZERLAND

CANTON SCHWYZ

We planned an entire summer trip one year around my father-in-law's desire to ride the steepest funicular in the world. This spectacular feat of engineering takes you up to the village of Stoos in the canton of Schwyz. Not only was the ride worthwhile, but I got to try a local potato dish there known as Ofeturli.

Nidwalden, Obwalden and Schwyz are known for their Ofeturli. Within these cantons, you will find numerous ways of making this dish, also sometimes referred to as *Ofetori, Ofenturli* or *Ofenguck*. Nidwalden and Obwalden tend to mix cheese with mashed potatoes that then gets placed in a casserole dish. After that, small batons of thick bacon are stabbed into the mashed potatoes before baking. Schwyz, particularly in the municipality of Einsiedeln, adds flour to their *Ofetori*. I have seen Einsiedler versions that mix the potatoes with flour to form a pastry base, which then gets topped with either bacon and onions like a tart, or filled with an egg and cheese mixture more like a quiche.

The 1935 book *Einsiedler Volksbräuche* (Einsiedler Folk Customs), about this community's traditions, describes children eagerly asking their mothers, *"Wän gits wiedr emoll Ofeturli?"* (When are we having Ofeturli again?) It says the answer given was that it would be made on January 6 for Dreikönigstag (Three Kings' Day) or January 21 for Meinradstag, a day honoring St. Meinrad, who in the 9th century first settled in the area that would eventually become the village of Einsiedeln with its Benedictine abbey. The book includes a simple recipe for this dish, described as a flatbread, made with potatoes, flour, butter, grated cheese and salt.

At the Restaurant Sternegg in Stoos, the Schwyzer Ofeturli arrived at our table on the sunny terrace. We were very hungry after hiking back from a climb up to the Fronalpstock summit. The floury potato cake with bacon had a light golden-brown layer of melted cheese with onions on its surface. This is the version of Ofeturli that I based my recipe on, with mushrooms for added flavor and texture. It tastes just as good on a summer's day in July as it does on a winter's day in January.

RÖSTI

FRIED GRATED POTATOES

Rösti is usually made by frying grated potatoes in a pan and forming them into a pancake. For this recipe, choose a waxy potato. These potatoes are lower in starch and higher in moisture. My recipe calls for butter, but clarified butter works especially well for making a crispy Rösti because it has a high smoke point.

Servings: 4

Prep: about 45 mins (incl. boiling the potatoes)
Cook: 20–30 mins

INGREDIENTS:

1 kg unpeeled, waxy potatoes (e.g., Yukon Gold or Annabelle) (2 ¼ lb)

2 teaspoons salt (for boiling the potatoes)

salt and pepper, to taste

3 tablespoons unsalted butter

SERVING SUGGESTIONS:

Geschnetzeltes mit Pilzen (p. 153), a fried egg or cheese, etc.

＊ **Curiosity:**
Swiss supermarkets label the bags of potatoes for "Rösti," so you know which ones to buy

INSTRUCTIONS:

1. Add the potatoes to a medium saucepan, cover them with water, add the salt and bring to a boil. When the potatoes are fork tender (but still a bit firm), place them in a colander to drain and cool.

2. Grate the potatoes into a large bowl. Season the grated potatoes with salt and pepper.

3. In a skillet with a diameter of about 26 cm (10 ¼ in), melt 2 tablespoons of butter over medium-high heat and spread it around evenly on the bottom. Then add the grated potatoes. Using a spatula, form them into a round pancake, pulling the potatoes away from the side of the skillet so they do not touch it. Cook for 10–15 minutes, until the potatoes turn crisp and golden brown.

4. Place a plate over the skillet and very carefully invert the potato pancake onto the plate. Add the remaining tablespoon of butter to the skillet, spreading it evenly across the bottom. Then, gently slide the potato pancake back into the pan. Cook for another 10–15 minutes, so the other side turns crisp and brown.

5. Serve immediately or place in a heated oven to keep it warm until you are ready to serve it.

Make-ahead tip:
For the best results, boil the potatoes and keep them in the fridge for 1–2 days.

SWITZERLAND'S SYMBOLIC POTATO DISH

THROUGHOUT SWITZERLAND

If you go for a hike in the Bernese Jura region or in parts of Neuchâtel, you have the chance to eat at historic farmhouse restaurants known as *métairies*. Many of the *métairies* only open for the summer, but some serve guests throughout the year. A typical meal at these mountain restaurants is Rösti, one of Switzerland's most iconic dishes.

As you may well know, the name of this dish is used to help describe an invisible line dividing the German- and French-speaking parts of the country. Known as the *Röstigraben* (Rösti ditch), this division goes beyond language to include such things as cultural differences and voting habits. According to the *Historisches Lexikon der Schweiz* (Historical Dictionary of Switzerland), the use of the term Graben in this context has existed since around the time of World War I, when these two regions of Switzerland aligned politically with the neighboring countries of France and Germany that matched them linguistically. The dictionary estimates that Rösti was combined with Graben in the 1970s, perhaps originating in German-speaking Switzerland. This theory works under the assumption that Rösti is more prevalent in cantons where German is primarily spoken. While this may be the case, you can certainly also find it in the French-speaking parts of the country.

To make Rösti, you grate the potatoes and fry them into a flat, round pancake. I would say that most people use potatoes that have already been boiled, perhaps a day or two in advance, but some people prefer raw potatoes. Ideally, when you cook the potatoes, they become crisp and golden brown on the outside while still a bit soft and almost creamy on the inside. When an American asks me about Rösti, I tell them the dish reminds me of hash browns in the US.

There are countless ways to prepare Rösti—with an egg, cheese, bacon, ham or mushrooms on top, or with a bratwurst or Geschnetzeltes (p. 153) on the side. When I make it in a frying pan, I invert it onto a plate to flip it while cooking. You can also try flipping it in the pan—just make sure to keep it off the floor!

SCHNETZ OND HÄPPERE
BAKED PEARS & POTATOES

These individual pots of sliced, baked pears and potatoes were inspired by a recipe from Lucerne, and its name reflects the regional dialect there. Seasoned with rosemary and topped with crunchy breadcrumbs, it makes for an easy side dish or light main dish for supper.

Servings: 4

Prep: about 15 mins
Bake: 25–35 mins

INGREDIENTS:

2 medium baking potatoes (e.g., Russet potatoes or Yukon Gold) (350 g)

2 pears for baking (e.g., Bosc or Williams) (250 g)

60 g Gruyère, grated (½ cup)

1 teaspoon dried rosemary

¼ teaspoon salt

freshly ground black pepper, to taste

2 tablespoons breadcrumbs (p. 17)

2 tablespoons unsalted butter, melted

TO GARNISH:

fresh parsley, finely chopped

INSTRUCTIONS:

1. Grease four 10 cm (4 in) oven-safe ramekins or cast-iron pots (0.2 liters each). Set aside.

2. Peel the potatoes and quarter them. Then slice them very thinly and place them in a large bowl. Next, halve, core and thinly slice the pears. Add them to the bowl with the potatoes, followed by the Gruyère, dried rosemary, salt and pepper, tossing all the ingredients together until they are well combined.

3. Add the pear and potato mixture to the greased pots. Sprinkle the surface with the breadcrumbs and then drizzle the melted butter evenly over the top.

4. Cover the dishes with their lids or aluminum foil and bake at 200°C (400°F) for 20–30 minutes. Then uncover the pots and continue baking for about 5–10 minutes more until the potatoes and pears are fully cooked and the surface has turned golden brown. Serve immediately in the pots.

PAIRING SWEET APPLES AND PEARS WITH POTATOES

CANTON LUCERNE

Like Valais with its Cholera—a pie filled with potatoes, apples and cheese—at least four other German-speaking cantons also have dishes combining sweet pip fruits with savory ingredients. The combination may seem surprising, but the flavor of the sweet apples and pears melds nicely with the potatoes. After all, one of the Swiss German words for potato is *Härdöpfel*, combining *Härd* (earth, as in soil) and *Öpfel* (apple). The same is true in French with *pomme de terre*, combining *pomme* (apple) and *de terre* (of the earth, also as in soil or ground).

Here are a few of these regional dishes from Aargau, Solothurn, Uri and Lucerne:

- **Schnitz und Drunder** (Aargau): A one-pot dish made by caramelizing sugar, which then gets cooked with potatoes, chopped salt pork, dried whole pears (Speckbirnen or Dörrbirnen) and dried apple slices. You will also find a version of this dish in Uri.

- **Funggi** (Solothurn): Essentially, this dish involves mashed potatoes mixed with mashed apples. You garnish it with crispy croutons to add some texture.

- **Birestunggis or Biräschtunggis** (Uri): This dish is similar to Funggi, except that it contains fresh pears, cooked and mashed with potatoes.

- **Schnetz ond Häppere** (Lucerne): In this canton, this dish is typically made with pears, much like the Aargauer version with bacon, but I also found a baked vegetarian version with apples, Öpfel und Häppere, in the 1977 Swiss cookbook by Marianne Kaltenbach, *Ächti Schwizer Chuchi* (Authentic Swiss Cuisine). I took inspiration from this recipe to develop my own version of this dish, using potatoes, pears and rosemary.

BLAUE ST. GALLER MIT BLAUSCHIMMELKÄSE

SMASHED BLUE ST. GALLER POTATOES WITH BLUE CHEESE

A modern take on Switzerland's Gschwellti (boiled potatoes), this recipe takes them one step further using the popular smashing technique. Keeping with the blue theme, I like these potatoes with blue cheese, but another semi-hard cheese will also work well.

Servings: 4

Prep: about 45 mins (incl. boiling the potatoes)
Bake: 30–40 mins

INGREDIENTS:

1 kg Blau St. Galler potatoes (2 ¼ lb)

2 teaspoons salt

2 tablespoons olive oil

200 g blue cheese (or other semi-hard cheese), sliced (7 oz)

TO GARNISH:

crème fraiche or sour cream

fresh parsley or cilantro, finely chopped

red chili, sliced (optiona)

salt and pepper, to taste

INSTRUCTIONS:

1. Place the potatoes in a pot with the salt. Add water until the potatoes are just covered. Over high heat, bring the water to a boil. Then reduce the heat slightly and cook until the potatoes are fork tender (20–40 minutes depending on their size).

2. Drain the potatoes and place them on a baking sheet lined with parchment paper. When the potatoes have cooled and are safe to touch, smash them with the palm of your hand. Then drizzle the potatoes with the olive oil. Bake at 200°C (400°F) for 20–30 minutes.

3. Take the pan out of the oven and top the potatoes with slices of blue cheese. Return them to the oven to bake for another 10 minutes or until the cheese has fully melted.

4. Take the pan out of the oven. Place a dollop of crème fraiche on each of the potatoes. Sprinkle the potatoes with parsley or cilantro and sliced red chili and season with salt and pepper. Serve immediately.

SMASHINGLY GOOD BLUE POTATOES

CANTON ST. GALLEN

The canton of St. Gallen lends its name to an exceptional blue potato that keeps its vivid color even when boiled, baked or fried. The Blau St. Galler is a relatively new potato variety, having only been approved for cultivation in Switzerland since 2006. Christoph Gämperli of the St. Gallische Saatzuchtgenossenschaft (St. Gallen seed breeding cooperative) led the creation of this new potato by crossing a Blue Swede potato with a Swiss heirloom variety, the Prättigauer potato from Graubünden.

My first encounter with this blue potato was at the Schlössli restaurant in the old city center of St. Gallen. As its name suggests, this restaurant is housed in a little castle, built during the 16th century. It has earned 14 Gault Millau points with a menu highlighting regional and sometimes forgotten produce, such as the medlar—a round brown fruit that needs to soften for a few weeks after harvesting (a process known as "bletting"). Ambros Wirth, the managing director of the restaurant, warmly welcomed our group when we entered

the historic dining room. One of the house specialties I got to taste that evening was a delicious Blau St. Galler potato soup served with bacon and a blue potato dumpling.

You can do almost anything with these potatoes, but I like to use the smashing technique that has you boil the unpeeled potatoes first and then smash them with the palm of your hand—a very satisfying task! You then cook them for a second time in the oven. I like the novelty as well as the taste of pairing these potatoes with a blue-veined cheese. In Switzerland, I often use Bleuchâtel from the canton of Neuchâtel, where I live. For a special treat, I make this dish with Jersey Blue, a buttery raw milk cheese from acclaimed cheesemaker Willi Schmid, also from the canton of St. Gallen.

STUPFETE

WARM HERBED VINAIGRETTE WITH BOILED POTATOES & CHEESE

Stupfete refers to a simple onion and herb vinaigrette thickened with flour. You serve this gently warmed sauce with boiled potatoes and a platter of cheese. The acidity of the Stupfete combined with the starchy potatoes and the smooth rich flavor of the cheese works wonderfully together.

Servings: 4–6

Prep: 30-45 mins (incl. boiling the potatoes)
Cook: about 15 mins

INGREDIENTS:

1 medium onion, finely chopped (½ cup)

1 clove garlic, minced

¼ teaspoon salt

½ teaspoon red chili flakes

1 tablespoon all-purpose flour

1 tablespoon unsalted butter

120 ml canola or rapeseed oil (½ cup)

80 ml apple cider vinegar (⅓ cup)

1 handful fresh dill and/or other fresh herbs, such as parsley or chives

freshy ground black pepper, to taste

SERVE WITH:

1 kg boiled potatoes (e.g. new potatoes) (2 ¼ lb)

assortment of cheeses, sliced

INSTRUCTIONS:

1. Put the onion, garlic, salt and chili flakes in a small bowl and toss with the flour until well combined. Melt the butter in a medium frying pan over medium heat. Add the onion and garlic mixture and cook the onion for about 5 minutes, until it becomes translucent. Then turn the heat down to low, stir in the oil and slowly simmer the onion and garlic for 8–10 minutes, stirring occasionally (do not let them turn brown).

2. Take the pan off the heat and stir in the vinegar until it becomes completely incorporated in the sauce. Then, stir in the fresh herbs. Season with pepper. Serve the vinaigrette warm or at room temperature. Spoon it onto your plate with boiled potatoes and sliced cheese.

A WARM VINAIGRETTE FOR BOILED POTATOES ON SUMMER NIGHTS

CANTON THURGAU

When I ask people from Switzerland to name their favorite Swiss dish, they normally say raclette or fondue. One time, the response surprised me because I had never heard of the dish! An author and journalist told me that her favorite was *Gschwellti*—pronounced something like, "g-shvell-ti". Honestly, I was embarrassed because I had never heard of it before and I asked her to write it down. Only afterwards did I realize that it appears on bags of potatoes at the supermarket.

Gschwellti is a Swiss German word that essentially means potatoes boiled in their skins. Living on the French-speaking side of the country, I use a much longer phrase to describe them—*les pommes de terre en robe des champs* (literally "potatoes in field dresses"). These are the potatoes that typically accompany a cheese fondue, such as Fondue à la Tomate (p. 69), or Raclette, a dish based on heating cheese and scraping off the melted part (*racler* in French means "to scrape"). Gschwellti can also be served with a platter of cheese. A typical condiment for this meal is *Quark* (*seré* in French)—a

soft, smooth dairy product with a light acidity—often mixed with some freshly chopped herbs.

The canton of Thurgau provides us with another type of condiment for boiled potatoes—a warm vinaigrette called Stupfete. In the Thurgauer dialect, *stupfe* means "to dip." Perhaps the dish is named this way because you dip your potatoes in the sauce. Historically, Stupfete was a summertime dish eaten by farmers at suppertime to replenish the salt lost during the day working in the fields. An early version of this dish was described in the *Schweizerisches Idiotikon*, a lexicon of the Swiss German language, as *"ein Gebräu von Essig, zerlassenem Schmalz und gerösteten Zwiebeln"* (a concoction of vinegar, melted lard and roasted onions). Modern recipes replace the lard with oil, as I have done.

This modest recipe is one of my favorites in this book, in part because it is ridiculously easy to prepare. I make it with lots of fresh dill and chili flakes. The acidity of the vinegar pairs well with the creamy boiled potatoes and the richness of the cheese.

RICE, PASTA, DUMPLINGS & MORE

This chapter takes you to all four linguistic regions of Switzerland, with a range of carbohydrate-laden dishes. The majority of these eight dishes originally came from mountainous regions, where mealtimes were historically simple, rustic dishes focused on replenishing calories after a hard day's work. My recipes and stories will give you a sense of the distinct characteristics and history of these regions, but also of their similarities. I designed the dishes to work as main courses for supper, but you could also serve them as side dishes.

To start, I have two rice recipes for you: Rys und Pohr (p. 99) from the canton of Uri, and Saffron Risotto (p. 103) from the canton of Ticino. In Ticino especially, you will find many different variations on risotto—with chestnuts, mushrooms or Merlot wine, for example. The country's shared border with Italy has certainly influenced these dishes.

After the rice dishes, there are some of my favorite pasta and dumpling recipes. The first comes from the canton of Obwalden and is a "backwards" version of Magronen, a rich Alpine recipe for macaroni and cheese (p. 107). Next, you can learn how to make buckwheat noodles (p. 111) found both in Ticino and Graubünden as well as in Italy. The three dumpling recipes that follow come from the Romansh-speaking region in Graubünden and French-speaking Valais.

The last recipe in this chapter, Chäs-Schoope (p. 127), will help you use up slightly stale bread, pairing it with cheese. In fact, every chapter in this book contains at least one recipe that calls for old bread or for breadcrumbs, which can be made from stale bread (p. 17).

You may have noticed that all the recipes in this chapter are vegetarian. Switzerland has a number of traditional recipes that are meatless by design, another aspect of Swiss suppers that I wanted to highlight.

RYS UND POHR

BAKED RICE & LEEKS

From the canton of Uri, this simple combination of rice, leeks and onions creates a really satisfying supper. I start this rice dish on the stove and then transfer it to the oven. You can make the crispy onions while the rice is baking.

Servings: 4

Prep: 15–20 mins
Bake: 30–35 mins

INGREDIENTS:

1–1 ¼ liters vegetable stock (p. 19) (4–5 cups)

1 tablespoon unsalted butter

1 tablespoon olive oil

1 medium onion, finely chopped (½ cup)

1 clove garlic, minced

350 g risotto rice (e.g., Arborio or Loto) (1 ½ cups)

60 ml dry white wine (e.g., Chasselas or Sauvignon Blanc) (¼ cup)

2 small leeks (white and green parts), thinly sliced (3 cups)

2 bay leaves

25 g Sbrinz (or Parmesan), grated (¼ cup)

salt and pepper, to taste

CRISPY ONIONS:

1 large onion, halved and thinly sliced (1 cup)

1-2 tablespoons all-purpose flour

1 pinch paprika

2-3 tablespoons unsalted butter

TO GARNISH:

fresh parsley, finely chopped

grated Sbrinz (or Parmesan)

INSTRUCTIONS:

1. In a medium saucepan, bring the vegetable stock to a simmer.

2. In a Dutch oven or other oven-safe pot that has an oven-safe cover, heat the butter and oil over medium heat on the stove. When the butter has melted, add the onion and garlic and cook for about 5 minutes, stirring frequently, until the onion becomes translucent.

3. Add the rice to the Dutch oven, stirring frequently to toast it for a few minutes. Pour in the wine and stir for a few minutes until it is absorbed. After that, stir in the chopped leeks, bay leaves and 1 liter (4 ¼ cups) of the warmed vegetable stock. Put the lid on and place it in an oven heated to 180°C (350°F). Bake for 30–35 minutes until the rice is al dente—softened but not mushy, slightly firm but not crunchy. While the rice bakes, prepare the crispy onions.

4. **Crispy onions:** Place the sliced onions in a bowl and toss them with the flour and paprika

until they are well coated. In a large frying pan, melt the butter over medium-high heat. Add half the onions and half the butter and fry them for 5–10 minutes, turning them occasionally, until they are browned and crispy. When done, transfer them to a plate covered with a paper towel to soak up the excess butter. Repeat this process with the remaining onions and butter.

5. When the rice is cooked, take the pan out of the oven and add the grated cheese. If you would like a creamier texture, stir in up to 250 ml (1 cup) of the remaining hot vegetable stock to the risotto. Season with salt and pepper.

6. Serve immediately by spooning the risotto onto individual plates or bowls and top with the grated cheese, crispy onions and parsley.

URI'S NOURISHING RICE WITH LEEKS

CANTON URI

At a press event early on in my blogging career, I met a journalist from the canton of Uri, one of Switzerland's three founding cantons. When I asked her about culinary specialties from this area, it surprised me when she described a risotto dish. I had always associated risotto with Ticino, Switzerland's Italian-speaking canton. How did German-speaking Uri become known for risotto?

If my knowledge of Swiss geography had been better at the time, I would have remembered that the southern part of Uri shares a border with Ticino. In addition, the Gotthard Pass connects Uri to Ticino and ultimately to Italy. Historically, the mountain pass played an important role as a transalpine route from northern to southern Europe, facilitating cultural and economic connections. You can find Italian influences not only in the cuisine of Uri but even in the architecture of Altdorf, its capital.

The risotto dish Rys und Pohr described by the Urner journalist is also known as *Ryys und Boor* and several other variations.

The names mean "rice and leeks." One theory on the origin of the dish connects it to the Italian miners who worked to build the Gotthard railway line in the late 19th century. You can imagine that this filling meal would be very satisfying at the end of a busy workday. Made without meat, it was apparently also popular during Lent.

Author Karl Iten includes a recipe for this dish in his 1972 cookbook, *Rezepte aus dem alten Uri* (recipes from old Uri), with a buttery onion sauce called *Belläschweitzi* (also called *Zwiebelschweitzi*). Unlike the crispy onions I have seen in more modern recipes, this sauce is poured over the risotto before serving. He also describes the custom of families gathering around the table to eat dishes like Rys und Pohr out of the same bowl.

I like this dish because it elevates simple, inexpensive ingredients to something special for a weeknight meal. Plus, baking it in the oven, rather than cooking it on the stove, allows you to focus on making those delicious crispy onions, which just might be my favorite part of this dish.

ⓙ RISOTTO ALLA MILANESE

SAFFRON RISOTTO WITH ROASTED TOMATOES

My version of this saffron risotto from the canton of Ticino includes a roasted tomato and red onion topping. It bakes in the oven while you stir the risotto in a pot on the stove.

Servings: 4

Prep: 20–30 mins
Cook: about 30 mins

INGREDIENTS:

ROASTED TOMATOES:

3–4 medium tomatoes, halved and quartered

1 medium red onion, halved and quartered

1 tablespoon olive oil

¼ teaspoon salt

RISOTTO:

1 tablespoon unsalted butter

1 tablespoon olive oil

1 medium onion, finely chopped (½ cup)

1 clove garlic, minced

400 g risotto rice (e.g., Arborio or Loto) (2 cups)

1 pinch saffron threads or powdered saffron

120 ml dry white wine (or vegetable stock) (½ cup)

1–1 ½ liters vegetable stock (p. 19), heated (4 to 6 cups)

25 g Sbrinz (or Parmesan), finely grated (¼ cup)

salt and pepper, to taste

TO GARNISH:

Sbrinz (or Parmesan), finely grated

fresh parsley, finely chopped

INSTRUCTIONS:

1. **Roast the tomatoes:** Place the tomatoes and onion on a baking sheet lined with parchment paper. Drizzle them with the oil and sprinkle with the salt. Toss them on the baking sheet to make sure they are completely coated in the oil. Roast in the oven for 25–30 minutes at 200°C (400°F) until they have softened. If they are ready before the risotto, keep them warm in the oven after it has been turned off.

2. **Cook the risotto:** Add the butter and olive oil to a medium saucepan over medium heat. When the butter has melted, add the onion and garlic and cook for about 5 minutes until they become translucent, stirring frequently.

3. Add the rice and saffron to the pan, stirring frequently to toast the rice for a few minutes. Then pour in the white wine, stirring until it becomes absorbed. After that, add 250 ml (1 cup) of hot vegetable stock and cook until the broth is nearly absorbed, stirring frequently to prevent sticking. Continue in this way, adding a cup at a time until the rice is cooked—it should still be slightly firm (al dente). This will take about 20 minutes.

4. Stir in the grated cheese. Add more hot vegetable stock if the risotto becomes too thick. Season with salt and pepper, as needed. Serve immediately in individual bowls, topping each with the roasted tomatoes and freshly chopped parsley, and more grated cheese if desired.

RISOTTO — ARGUABLY TICINO'S MOST POPULAR DISH

CANTON TICINO

After visiting the Naretto bakery in Ascona for a loaf of Pane Valle Maggia, one of my favorite Swiss breads, I continued walking to the Terreni alla Maggia farm and winery—the birthplace of 100% Swiss-grown rice, first harvested in 1997. There, I bought rice to make one of Ticino's most emblematic dishes, saffron risotto (a.k.a. Risotto alla Milanese or Risotto allo zafferano).

Risotto of all varieties shows up everywhere in the canton of Ticino—from the family supper table to carnival celebrations. The dish can also be found in Michelin-starred restaurants, such as Locanda Barbarossa at Castello del Sole, the luxury resort adjacent to Terreni alla Maggia. This restaurant cooks with rice grown on the farm next to the hotel. The farm also has a shop open to the public, where you can buy risotto, polenta, wine and other local products to take home.

Why is Risotto alla Milanese, named after an Italian city, a traditional dish in Ticino? The answer is that this canton did not always belong to Switzerland. It was part of the Duchy of Milan until it joined the Swiss confederation in the early 16th century. Linguistic, cultural and economic connections between Ticino and Italy have certainly led to similarities when it comes to food.

In Milan, a popular legend attributes the origin of saffron risotto to a wedding in 1574. Apparently, a craftsman working with stained glass in the Duomo di Milano, Milan's landmark cathedral, used saffron to give his windowpanes a yellow tint. Stories differ as to whether it was intentional or accidental, but during a wedding banquet at the cathedral, somehow some of his saffron ended up in the risotto—much to everyone's delight—and the practice has continued to this day.

While we do not know exactly how Risotto alla Milanese arrived in Ticino, it is now considered a typical dish there. You will find it served with *luganighe* (a raw pork sausage) or its smaller version, the *luganighetta*. A risotto that was once fit for a wedding banquet in Milan can today make a weeknight supper extra special.

⑳ HINDERSI-MAGRONEN
BACKWARDS MACARONI & CHEESE

My recipe is based on a regional version of the classic Swiss Älplermagronen (Alpine macaroni and cheese). You make it with browned onions, diced potatoes and cheese, all cooked in the same pot. Serve with applesauce for the full Alpine experience.

Servings: 4

Prep: 15–20 mins
Cook: about 30 mins

INGREDIENTS:

2 tablespoons unsalted butter

1 large onion, finely chopped (1 cup)

1 large potato, peeled and finely diced (1 cup)

500 g macaroni (1 lb)

about 1 liter vegetable stock (p. 19) (4 ¼ cups)

100 ml light cream (scant ½ cup)

200 ml milk (generous ¾ cup)

150 g Sbrinz (or Parmesan), grated (5 oz)

150 g Gruyère (or other cheese), grated (5 oz)

salt and pepper, to taste

TO GARNISH:

grated Sbrinz (or Parmesan)

parsley, finely chopped

SERVING SUGGESTION:

applesauce

INSTRUCTIONS:

1. Melt the butter over medium-high heat in a large, deep frying pan. Add the onions, reduce the heat to medium and cook for 15–20 minutes, stirring frequently, until they turn dark brown.

2. Add the potatoes to the pan, spreading them into an even layer and cook them for a few minutes. Then add the macaroni on top. Pour in enough vegetable stock to just cover the pasta and bring to a boil. Then reduce the heat slightly, cover the pan and cook for 8–10 minutes until the pasta and potatoes are cooked.

3. Pour in the cream and milk, and bring the mixture to a boil. Then sprinkle in the cheese. Stir everything together over low to medium heat until the cheese has fully melted and created a smooth sauce. Season with salt and pepper. Serve immediately, garnished with parsley and cheese, with applesauce on the side.

OBWALDEN'S BACKWARDS MACARONI AND CHEESE

CANTON OBWALDEN

Why do the Obwaldeners refer to their local version of Alpine macaroni and cheese as *hindersi* (backwards)? Because the way they make their regional version of Älplermagronen differs in a few important ways. I traveled to an elevation of 1,538 meters (5,046 ft) on the Fluonalp to taste it for myself.

Apparently, the canton of Obwalden had an ongoing macaroni rivalry with their neighboring canton of Nidwalden. A legend describes how long ago, the villagers of Engelberg were transporting their secret recipe for Hindersi-Magronen to the village of Kerns in a horse-drawn carriage. During their journey, a band of intrepid Nidwaldners attacked the carriage and tried to steal the recipe. Thankfully for the steadfast Obwaldners, the recipe arrived intact.

The backwards aspect of the Obwaldner's version of macaroni and cheese refers to how the onions are cooked, and because the pasta is added to the pot before the liquid. The onions brown in butter, giving the macaroni a slightly darker hue. A more

typical Älplermagronen has crispy onions sprinkled on top. The convenient one-pot method results from being prepared on the Alp—they lacked space for multiple pots and fires.

This is how they prepare it at the mountain *Beizli* (tavern) on Fluonalp. I sat down for supper that evening, eagerly anticipating my macaroni. It arrived in a large wooden bowl with the traditional wooden spoon. The cook had sprinkled a generous amount of Sbrinz cheese on top. The server told me that they make their macaroni with equal portions of Sbrinz and Alpkäse (Alp cheese). It came with a bowl of applesauce, the customary accompaniment.

The Schnider family have been operating the cheese dairy at Fluonalp for three generations. In addition to the *Beizli*, they also offer overnight accommodation, which I took advantage of. In the morning, I hiked down the mountain, back to the town of Giswil to catch my trains to Neuchâtel. I feel very lucky to have tasted the real Hindersi-Magronen. When I make this recipe at home, I am reminded of the beautiful sunrise on the Alp.

21 PIZZOCCHERI

BUCKWHEAT NOODLES WITH VEGETABLES

A very hearty vegetarian dish, Pizzoccheri is found in Switzerland's Italian-speaking regions. Do not be intimidated by this recipe—you can make these rustic buckwheat noodles easily on your kitchen counter with a rolling pin and a sharp knife (p. 112). Cabbage is traditionally added to this dish, but when in season, I like using kale.

Servings: 4–6

Prep: about 30 mins
Cook: 15–30 mins

INGREDIENTS:

2 medium potatoes, peeled and finely diced (2 cups)

1 tablespoon olive oil

1 tablespoon unsalted butter

1 small onion (½ cup), finely chopped

1 clove garlic, minced

1 carrot, grated (½ cup)

1 small bunch fresh sage, sliced thinly

Pizzoccheri noodles (p. 112)

250 ml dry white wine (e.g., Chasselas or Sauvignon Blanc) or vegetable stock (1 cup)

200 g kale or Savoy cabbage, chopped (7 oz)

salt and pepper, to taste

TO GARNISH:

Sbrinz (or Parmesan) cheese, grated

Alpkäse (Alp cheese) or Gruyère, grated

INSTRUCTIONS:

1. Bring a large pot of salted water to a boil. Add the potatoes and cook them for 5–7 minutes. While the potatoes are cooking, add the butter and olive oil to a large skillet over medium heat.

2. When the butter has melted, add the onion and garlic. Cook for about 5 minutes, stirring frequently, until the onion becomes transparent. Then add the carrots and sage to the skillet and cook for several minutes, stirring frequently.

3. When the potatoes are almost done, add the Pizzoccheri noodles to the same pot and cook until the noodles rise to the surface (5–7 minutes). After you add the Pizzoccheri to the water, add the wine (or stock) to the skillet, increasing the heat to medium high. Then add the kale or cabbage, place a lid on the skillet and steam for a few minutes until these vegetables soften. Take the lid off and turn the heat down to low to keep it warm until the Pizzoccheri are ready.

4. When the potatoes are tender and the Pizzoccheri have risen to the surface fully cooked, use a slotted spoon to drain them and transfer them to the skillet with the vegetables. Stir everything together and season with salt and pepper. Serve immediately, sprinkled generously with the grated cheese.

HANDMADE PIZZOCCHERI NOODLES

Pizzoccheri is a type of short tagliatelle, a flat ribbon pasta. This recipe makes the noodles you will need for the recipe above.

Servings: 8

Prep: 1 hour (incl. time for the dough to rest)

INGREDIENTS:

250 g buckwheat flour
(scant 2 cups)

100 g all-purpose flour
(⅔ cup + 3 tablespoons)

1 teaspoon salt

200 ml water
(¾ cup + 1 tablespoon)

INSTRUCTIONS:

1. In a large bowl, whisk together the two types of flour and salt. Make a well in the center of the bowl and pour in the water. Stir everything together to form a dough. Let the dough rest for 30 minutes.

2. On a lightly floured surface, roll out the dough to 2–3 mm (⅒ in) thick. Dust the rolling pin with flour if the dough starts to stick to it. Then drag a sharp knife through the dough to cut the Pizzoccheri. They should have a width of 4–5 mm (about ⅕ in) and a length of 10 cm (4 in).

Make-ahead tips:
Prepare the Pizzoccheri dough in the morning and refrigerate it until you are ready to use it in the evening.

Alternatively, make the noodles, dust them with flour, spread them out on a baking sheet covered with parchment paper and dusted with flour, cover them and refrigerate for to 2–3 days until you are ready to cook them.

SWISS ITALIAN BUCKWHEAT NOODLES

CANTONS
GRAUBÜNDEN
AND TICINO

Albergo-Ristorante Croce Bianca in Poschiavo has made a strong commitment to serving dishes made with local ingredients. This restaurant, along with others in the Valposchiavo region of Graubünden, have signed the Charta 100% Valposchiavo—a pledge to have at least three dishes on their menu that are made with only local ingredients. Already known for having nearly all its farmland certified as organic, this Italian-speaking valley currently has more than a dozen restaurants that have signed the charter. One of the dishes at the Croce Bianca restaurant that fulfils the criteria is the Pizzoccheri alla Poschiavina. They describe it as a buckwheat tagliatelle with potatoes, vegetables and a garlic-sage butter.

The canton of Ticino is also a destination for Pizzoccheri. When I arrived at the big Saturday market in Bellinzona one day in autumn, the first food truck I saw was selling plates of these buckwheat noodles. In fact, Valtellina—just across the border in the northern Italian region of Lombardy—is recognized as being the birthplace of this dish.

Even though it does not contain meat, this wholesome dish is quite filling. Often layered with cheese, I prefer to only sprinkle cheese on top. It makes the dish a bit lighter and I find that the flavor of the buckwheat and vegetables is also more pronounced.

In Switzerland, you can purchase pre-made, dried Pizzoccheri noodles, but you can also prepare them at home. You just need a little patience, a sharp knife and a rolling pin. The taste of fresh pasta, as well as the satisfaction of having made it yourself, is certainly worth it.

㉒ CAPUNET

LITTLE SPINACH DUMPLINGS WITH ROASTED TOMATO SAUCE

These tasty spinach dumplings are typically served with grated cheese. For a spin on this traditional recipe, I serve them with a roasted tomato and red pepper sauce (recipe at cuisinehelvetica.com). To save time, make both the sauce and the Capunet in advance.

Servings: 4

Prep: about 60 mins
(incl. resting time for the batter)
Cook: 20–30 mins

INGREDIENTS:

500 g fresh spinach (1 lb)

2–3 tablespoons unsalted butter

I large onion, finely chopped
(1 cup)

1 clove garlic, minced

2 tablespoons fresh basil, chopped

250 g all-purpose flour (2 cups)

25 g breadcrumbs (p. 17) (¼ cup)

1 teaspoon salt

¼ teaspoon nutmeg

freshly ground black pepper, to taste

2 large eggs

SERVING SUGGESTION:

Roasted tomato sauce or your favorite tomato-based pasta sauce

TO GARNISH:

Sbrinz (or Parmesan), grated

INSTRUCTIONS:

1. Bring a large pot of salted water to a boil. Blanch the spinach until just wilted. Then immediately place the spinach in a colander and rinse with cold water.

2. Melt 1–2 tablespoons of butter in a medium frying pan over medium heat. Cook the onions and garlic for about 5 minutes until the onions become translucent. Then, puree the spinach, onion-garlic mixture and fresh basil with an upright or immersion blender until smooth (add additional water, as needed). Set aside.

3. In a large bowl, whisk together the flour, breadcrumbs, salt, nutmeg and pepper. Make a well in the center and add the eggs and pureed spinach mixture. Stir everything together vigorously until well-combined and the batter starts to pull away from the sides of the bowl. Cover the bowl and let the batter rest for 30 minutes at room temperature.

4. Bring a large pot of salted water to a rolling boil. Place a large scoop of the batter on a cutting board. With a table knife, carefully scrape small, thin pieces of the batter—about 3 cm (1 ¼ in) in length—directly into the boiling water. When the dumplings float to the top after a few minutes, use a slotted spoon

to remove them and place them in a colander to drain. Then transfer them to the frying pan (see step 5). Repeat this process until you have used all the batter.

5. Melt 1–2 tablespoons of butter in a large frying pan over medium heat. After each batch of dumplings has drained, add them to the pan, stirring occasionally.

6. Serve the Capunet in a puddle of the tomato sauce and sprinkle with a generous amount of grated cheese.

   Variation: Skip the tomato sauce altogether and just toss the Capunet in the frying pan with some grated cheese.

   Make-ahead tips:
   Prepare the Capunet in advance and store them in the refrigerator for 1–2 days.

   You can also freeze the Capunet after you make them. Spread them out on a baking sheet lined with parchment paper and put them in the freezer. Once they have frozen, put them in a sealed container and return them to the freezer.

FORTIFYING LITTLE SPINACH DUMPLINGS FROM VALPOSCHIAVO

CANTON
GRAUBÜNDEN

One of my favorite ways to spend a day in Switzerland is hiking and eating. Thankfully, various regional culinary walks make this possible—they take you on foot through vineyards, valleys, cities and mountainous areas, with stops along the way for food and drink. When you check in for the walk, you sometimes receive a pouch to wear around your neck that holds a wine glass. It looks a bit silly, but everyone does it, so it somehow feels natural—and it reduces waste by avoiding plastic throwaway glasses.

I discovered Capunet during one such event, the straMangiada, in the canton of Graubünden's Valposchiavo region. Held in early July, straMangiada—a blend of *strada* (road) and *mangiare* (eat)—features 10 stands with food and drink along a seven-kilometer route from the village of Le Prese to Poschiavo.

Valposchiavo is on the route of the Bernina Express railway line, a UNESCO World Heritage site that passes through an astounding 55 tunnels and over 196 bridges. This Italian-speaking valley is

one of four in Graubünden. It has its own flavor of Swiss Italian specialties, such as Pizzoccheri (p.111).

On the walk, I tasted local wines, Alpine cheese, dried meats, grilled sausages and more. The plate of cheesy Capunet appeared at one of the last stops. These little spinach dumplings reminded me of gnocchi, Spätzli or Knöpfli (p. 115). Some recipes include potatoes, others make Capunet with nettles or wild spinach. Served up by a local soccer team all wearing yellow hats, the little plate of fortifying dumplings was one of my favorite dishes on the route.

Traditionally, Capunet are only served with cheese, but I adapted the recipe to include a roasted tomato and red pepper sauce. It lightens the dish a little, but you should still cover it with cheese, especially if you can get some directly from this spectacular region.

CAPUNS

SWISS CHARD WRAPPED DUMPLINGS

My vegetarian version of these Swiss chard-wrapped dumplings contains sun-dried tomatoes. This hearty dish takes some time, so you may want to save it for a weekend supper unless you make the dumplings in advance.

Servings: 4–5 (14–16 dumplings)

Prep: about 30 mins
Cook: 40–45 mins

INGREDIENTS:

CAPUNS:

200 g all-purpose flour (1 ⅔ cups)

½ teaspoon salt

2 large eggs, lightly beaten

100 ml milk (scant ½ cup)

65 g sun–dried tomatoes in oil, finely chopped (⅓ cup)

1 small handful fresh chives and/or parsley, finely chopped

zest ½ organic lemon

8–10 large stalks of Swiss chard, leaves only*

*There is a large variation in the size of Swiss chard leaves. You can generally make two Capuns out of one large leaf but only one out of a smaller leaf. If you have smaller Swiss chard, you may need a total of 16–20 leaves.

BROTH:

1 tablespoon unsalted butter

1 large onion, finely chopped (1 cup)

stalks from the Swiss chard leaves used for the Capuns, finely chopped (about 1 cup)

1 carrot, finely grated (½ cup)

1 clove garlic, minced

1 teaspoon dried basil

1 teaspoon salt

750 ml water (3 cups)

180 ml light cream (¾ cup)

freshly ground black pepper, to taste

piment d'Espelette (or cayenne pepper), to taste

TO GARNISH:

Bergkäse or Alpkäse cheese (or Sbrinz, Gruyère, Emmentaler), grated

INSTRUCTIONS:

1. **Prepare the filling for the Capuns.** In a large bowl, whisk together the flour and salt. Make a well in the center and add the lightly beaten eggs, milk and sun-dried tomatoes. With a spoon, stir all the ingredients together until the flour is completely incorporated. Then stir vigorously until the runny dough starts to pull away from the sides of the bowl and the mixture becomes smooth without lumps. Stir in the fresh herbs and lemon zest. Cover the bowl and set aside.

2. **Prepare the broth.** Melt the butter in a large frying pan over medium heat. Add the onion, chopped Swiss chard stalks, grated carrot and garlic to the pan. Cook for about 5 minutes or until the onions become translucent. Then stir in the dried basil and salt. Add the water and bring to a boil. Then reduce the heat, cover the pan and let the broth simmer for 20–30 minutes while you prepare the Swiss chard leaves. Season with pepper and piment d'Espelette, as desired.

3. **Prepare the Swiss chard leaves.** Bring a large pot of salted water to a boil. Get a large bowl of ice water ready. Add the Swiss chard leaves to the boiling water and blanch each leaf for about 30 seconds. Transfer them straight from the boiling water into the ice water. Then place the cooled leaves in a colander to drain. After that, wrap them in a clean kitchen towel to dry them.

4. **Assemble the Capuns.** Take one of the Swiss chard leaves (or half of one of the leaves if they are large) and lay it out flat. Add 1–2 tablespoons of filling to one end of the leaf. Start rolling up the leaf around the filling, folding in the sides as you go to create a little dumpling package. Set the dumpling on a plate and continue until you have used up all the filling.

5. **Cook the Capuns.** Add the Capuns to the simmering broth, cover the pan and cook for about 10 minutes over medium-high heat, turning them over about halfway through. Next, stir in the cream until it is well-combined and heated through. Serve the Capuns with the broth in low bowls, sprinkled with grated cheese and fresh parsley.

Make-ahead tip:
Prepare the Capuns in the morning and let them sit in the refrigerator until suppertime. Make sure not to stack them, or the filling might start to seep out.

SWISS CHARD PACKAGES FROM GRAUBÜNDEN

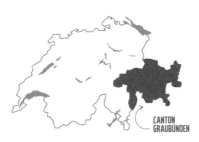

CANTON
GRAUBÜNDEN

Capuns exist in many different forms. The essential component of this dish is a dumpling batter wrapped in a chard leaf. These chard packages are usually served in a vegetable or meat broth, with or without cream. Cured meats, such as *Salsiz* (salami), *Bündnerfleisch* (air-dried beef) or bacon can be in the filling, served on top, or both. In addition, you can find vegetarian versions of this dish, made with mushrooms or sun-dried tomatoes, for example.

The type of chard used can vary as well. In Graubünden, the smaller, tender *Schnittmangold* (cut chard) leaves—also known as *Blattmangold* (leaf chard)—are traditionally used for Capuns. You can similarlyuse *Krautstiel* (cabbage stem in German), also known as *Stielmangold* (stem chard), which has large green leaves with thick white stalks, or long, thin stalks in red and golden hues.

English speakers know this leafy vegetable as Swiss chard. It is not clear why "Swiss" is part of the name since chard is not native to Switzerland. One theory is that it was named after Swiss botanist Gaspard Bauhin from Basel because he was the first to describe chard. Another theory connects the discovery to German botanist Karl Heinrich Emil Koch, but he was not even Swiss. I have also read that seed merchants from the Netherlands wanted to differentiate it from French spinach varieties, so they added "Swiss" to the name.

Today, you will find Capuns in many regions of Graubünden. One legend ties this dish to the tiny mountain village of Camuns. As described in an article published online by Radiotelevisiun Svizra Rumantscha (a Swiss Romansh broadcaster), a woman from the village supposedly created this dish in the late 18th century. She made it with what little ingredients she had left after Russian troops led by General Suvorov passed through the village in a failed effort to drive out the French from Switzerland. Suvorov may not have been successful with his campaign, but the Capuns have become a beloved cantonal dish.

SWEET POTATO GUYENËFLES

LITTLE SWEET POTATO DUMPLINGS WITH BRUSSELS SPROUTS

Guyenëfles are little dumpling-noodles boiled in salted water. Instead of making them with potatoes, I have used sweet potatoes. Topped with roasted Brussels sprouts and hazelnuts, this dish works well for an easy weeknight supper if you make the Guyenëfles ahead of time.

Servings: 4

Prep: about 1 hour (incl. time for the batter to rest)
Cook: 30–45 mins

INGREDIENTS:

GUYENËFLES:

200 g roasted sweet potatoes, pureed (7 oz)

300 g all-purpose flour (2 ½ cups)

2 teaspoons salt

1 pinch nutmeg

freshly ground black pepper, to taste

3 large eggs

100 ml milk (scant ½ cup)

100 ml water (scant ½ cup)

1–2 tablespoons unsalted butter

50 g Gruyère (or other cheese), grated (scant ½ cup)

60 ml light cream (¼ cup)

ROASTED BRUSSELS SPROUTS:

500 g Brussels sprouts, cleaned and halved (1 lb)

2 tablespoons olive oil

salt, to taste

TO GARNISH:

toasted hazelnuts, roughly chopped

Gruyère cheese, grated

INSTRUCTIONS:

1. **Roast the sweet potatoes.** Place the whole, unpeeled sweet potatoes on a baking sheet lined with parchment paper. Bake at 200°C (400°F) for 40–60 minutes or until tender. Peel the sweet potatoes and puree the flesh with an upright or immersion blender or mash them until smooth.

2. **Prepare the batter:** Whisk together the flour, salt, nutmeg and pepper in a large bowl. In another large bowl, whisk together the sweet potato puree, eggs, milk and water until well combined. Make a well in the center of the flour mixture. Pour the wet ingredients into the well. Stir all the ingredients together until the flour is completely incorporated. Then stir vigorously until the batter starts to pull away from the sides of the bowl as you mix. Cover the bowl and let the batter sit at room temperature for about 30 minutes.

3. **Prepare the Brussels sprouts:** Line a baking sheet with parchment paper. Place the Brussels sprouts on the baking sheet and drizzle them with the oil and sprinkle with salt. Bake for 15–20 minutes at 200°C (400°F). While the Brussels sprouts are in the oven, prepare the guyenëfles.

4. **Make the guyenëfles:** Bring a pot of salted water to a boil. Place the Knöpflisieb or Spätzlisieb (Knöpfli or Spätzli maker) over the boiling water. Add large spoonfuls of the dough to the Knöpfli/Spätzli-maker so they

fall into the boiling water. Remove them with a slotted spoon when they float to the top of the water, after a few minutes of cooking. Place them in a colander to drain.

(Please note: If you do not have a Knöpfli/Spätzli-maker, you can also use a metal colander with large holes and push the batter through them into the boiling water or use the cutting–board method described in the Capunet recipe, p. 115).

5. Melt the butter in a large frying pan over medium-high heat. Add the guyenëfles and toss them until they are fully warmed and lightly browned. Stir in the cheese and cream to create a smooth sauce. Serve topped with the roasted Brussels sprouts and garnished with the grated cheese and chopped hazelnuts.

Make-ahead tips:
Prepare the sweet potato puree in advance. Store it in the refrigerator for 2–3 days until you are ready to use it.

Make the guyenëfles in advance. Once they are cooked, you can drain them and store them in the refrigerator for 2–3 days.

Freeze the guyenëfles. You can also freeze them after you cook them. Spread them out on a baking sheet lined with parchment paper and put them in the freezer. Once they have frozen, put them in a sealed container and return them to the freezer.

CELEBRATING LOCAL DIALECTS WITH ALPINE DUMPLINGS

CANTON VALAIS

Before I moved to Switzerland, I had only a vague awareness of the German *Spätzle* (*Spätzli* in Switzerland; literally "little sparrow"), and I had certainly never heard of *Knöpfli* (literally "little buttons"), another version of these little boiled dumpling-noodles. You can use the same thick batter to make them both—the only difference is their shape and size. Spätzli are longer and thinner, while *Knöpfli* are smaller and have a more rounded shape. You make them by cutting off individual pieces of the wet dough from a cutting board straight into a pot of boiling water, or you can use a *Spätzlisieb* or *Knöpflisieb*. The *Spätzli* or *Knöpfli* are formed by pressing the dough through this special utensil with small holes (your colander might also work for this task).

In the French-speaking regions of Valais, they call their version *guyenëfles* or *quyenèfle*, which sounds something like "keh-nuh-fluh,"—essentially like a French pronunciation of *Knöpfli*. They are also referred to as *knoefli* or *quyenèfle*. These terms come from the Lower Valais patois, a dialect that has been recognized by Switzerland's Federal Office of Culture as one of the country's living traditions.

If there are no potatoes in the guyenëfles batter, potatoes could be served alongside them, as described in the 1993 book, *Assiettes valaisannes: nourritures d'hier et d'avant-hier* (Valais plates: food from yesterday and the day before).

Switzerland has multiple regional variations of these dishes. The canton of Glarus has the *Zogglä*, traditionally made with potatoes, like gnocchi. Some grated Schabziger, a green-colored cheese flavored with fenugreek will often be added to this dish. In Aargau, they make *Härdöpfel-Chnöpfli*, also with potatoes, and in Graubünden, they have *Pizokel*, sometimes made with buckwheat flour.

I love the versatility of these humble dishes because you can add ingredients to both the batter and the finished dumplings to completely change their taste and texture. And when you make this dish at home, you make a small gesture toward keeping these old recipes alive.

25 CHÄS-SCHOOPE

PAN-FRIED BREAD & CHEESE

This super quick pan-fried bread and cheese supper could not be simpler to make. I like serving it alongside some pickles or spicy kimchi to help cut the richness of the cheese. I am sure you will make this dish again and again!

Servings: 2–4

Prep: about 10 mins
Cook: 10–15 mins

INGREDIENTS:

250 g stale crusty bread, cut into about 3 cm (1 in) cubes (¼ lb)

3–4 tablespoons unsalted butter

150 g Appenzeller, Gruyère or other cheese, grated (1 ¼ cups)

60 ml milk (¼ cup)*

black pepper, to taste

*For a richer version of this dish, use the same quantity of light cream instead of milk.

TO GARNISH:

paprika or pimentón (Spanish smoked paprika) (optional)

fresh parsley or chives, finely chopped

INSTRUCTIONS:

1. Melt 2 tablespoons of butter in a large skillet over medium-high heat. When it has fully melted, add the cubed bread. Toss the bread in the butter and toast the pieces for 5–8 minutes until they become light golden brown, turning occasionally. Add additional butter, as needed, depending on how dry the bread is.

2. While the bread is toasting, add the grated cheese, milk and pepper to a large bowl. Stir everything together until well combined.

3. When the bread has toasted, add the cheese mixture to the skillet and stir continuously until the cheese has fully melted. Serve immediately garnished with parsley or chives and a sprinkle of paprika (optional).

APPENZELL'S SUPER QUICK SKILLET FONDUE

APPENZELL REGION

When my son and I made this dish for the first time, we were incredulous. Why had we not thought of making this before? It is so easy! You simply fry cubes of stale bread in a pan with some butter, milk and cheese.

In the Appenzell region, they call this dish Appenzeller Chäs-Schoope. "Chäs," is the Swiss German word for cheese. According to the *Schweizerisches Idiotikon*, a lexicon of the Swiss German language, "Schoope" means jacket. I have also seen a similar dish from Appenzell that goes by the name, Alte Maa (old man). The canton of Graubünden has a dish known as Chäsgetschäder. It has a higher proportion of milk and other liquids such as bouillon or wine, so the bread has a mushier consistency.

In Appenzell, the cheese used for this dish would obviously be Appenzeller. Known as the "spiciest cheese in Switzerland," they have been making it in eastern Switzerland for over 700 years. It often appears in posters at train stations, featuring three men in traditional clothing holding an index finger vertically over their mouths to indicate

they are keeping quiet. Why? Because the recipe for the herbal brine used to make this cheese is top secret!

Charly Gmünder, the former owner of the Baren Hotel Restaurant in Gonten, was well known for serving Chäs-Schoope at his establishment. He lent his recipe to the famous cookbook series for children that stars a blue parrot named Globi. For this dish, he calls for equal parts bread and cheese. Another recipe I came across instructs you to use a quantity of butter equal to 50% of the weight of the bread! I am sure these versions are all wonderful to eat, nonetheless for a weeknight meal, I reduced the milk fat content by using less butter and cheese, and milk instead of cream. You can think of this dish as a super-quick skillet fondue, and a delicious way to use up old bread and leftover pieces of cheese.

STEWS
& MEAT DISHES

For multiple reasons, since moving from the US to Switzerland in 2012, I have reduced the amount of meat I cook at home, both in quantity and frequency. If you are doing the same, there are two recipes in this chapter that you can turn into vegetarian dishes: You can make the Omeletten (p. 157) with a vegetable filling and you can prepare the Geschnetzeltes mit Pilzen (p. 153) entirely with mushrooms.

Some dishes in this chapter are known throughout Switzerland, such as Zürcher Geschnetzeltes. This is traditionally made with sliced veal and mushrooms, but my recipe for Geschnetzeltes calls for beef tenderloin instead. Other dishes, such as Fricassée Genevoise—a recipe for braised pork in red wine, linked to the canton of Geneva (p. 133)—are only known in the region they come from.

I start out with four recipes that take some time, making them more suitable for weekend suppers. Three of these dishes involve cooking the meat for several hours until it becomes tender: Fricassée Genevoise; Stunggis, a pork and cabbage stew found in the canton of Nidwalden (p. 137) and Osso Buco from Ticino (p. 141). The fourth dish, Jacquerie Neuchâteloise (p. 145), requires you to slowly cook sauerkraut with caraway seeds and juniper berries. This recipe from the canton of Neuchâtel is usually made with snails, but I use chicken instead.

The second half of the chapter features less-time intensive recipes that are easy weeknight meals, such as Riz Casimir, a retro chicken curry that is a childhood favorite of many (p. 149). I end with Steak Vigneron—a seasoned hamburger sandwich (p. 165) from the canton of Neuchâtel—along with a recipe for the bread rolls to make it with (p.166).

26 FRICASSÉE GENEVOISE

BRAISED PORK IN RED WINE

To make this braised pork dish, you first let the meat soak in a red wine marinade for about 24 hours. The tender pork and full-bodied sauce go very well with creamy mashed potatoes.

Servings: 4

Prep: 10 mins + 24 hours for marinating
Cook: 1 ½–2 hours

INGREDIENTS:

MARINADE:

600 g boneless stewing pork (e.g., pork shoulder), cut into 5 cm (2 in) chunks (1 lb)

1 large onion, quartered

3 whole cloves

1 carrot, halved

3 juniper berries (optional)

5 whole black peppercorns

2 cloves garlic, peeled and halved

2 bay leaves

1 sprig fresh thyme

1 small bunch fresh sage

750 ml light red wine (e.g., Gamay, Beaujolais or Pinot Noir) (3 cups)

OTHER INGREDIENTS:

½ teaspoon salt

2 tablespoons all-purpose flour

1 tablespoon unsalted butter

2 tablespoons light cream

freshly ground black pepper, to taste

SERVING SUGGESTIONS:

mashed potatoes or buttered egg noodles

INSTRUCTIONS:

1. Add the pork chunks to a medium bowl. Pierce the onion pieces with the cloves and place them in the bowl. Then add the remaining marinade ingredients and stir everything together. Cover the bowl and refrigerate, allowing the pork to marinate for approximately 24 hours.

2. Remove the pork chunks from the marinade and place them in a separate bowl. Sprinkle the pork with the salt and flour and stir to completely coat the meat in the flour.

3. Pass the marinade through a sieve, discarding the ingredients that remain. Add the strained marinade to a medium saucepan and bring to a boil. Lower the heat and simmer for about 15 minutes, until the marinade reduces by about one-third. Take the pan off the heat and set aside. While the marinade is reducing, brown the pork.

4. Melt the butter over medium-high heat in a medium cast iron frying pan or braising pan. Cook the pork chunks on all sides until browned. Then add the reduced marinade to the pot and bring to a boil. Lower the temperature, cover the pan and let the pork simmer for about 1 ½ hours or until the meat is tender. Stir in the light cream, season with salt and pepper and serve immediately.

GENEVA'S BLOODY PORK STEW

CANTON GENÈVE

The first time I heard the word *fricassée* was while watching Bugs Bunny cartoons as a child in the US. To avoid being shot, Bugs Bunny described himself as a "fricasseeing rabbit," a type of rabbit that requires a special hunting license that Elmer Fudd, who is chasing him, does not have.

The term fricassée has several meanings. In English, it refers to meat or poultry cooked in a white, creamy sauce. French-speaking Switzerland also uses the word but to describe a cut of pork spareribs from the front part of the pig's rib cage where it meets the shoulder. You will also see fricassée used in Geneva for its Fricassée Genevoise—pork braised in red wine (Vaud has its own version too). This dish is traditionally made with pork ribs.

Historically, fricassée was also used more broadly to describe the pieces of pork you shared with family, neighbors and friends after the autumn slaughter. You can see vestiges of this tradition in the canton of Jura's feast of Saint Martin in November. Long ago, farmers smoked and cured meat for the winter, but they still had an abundance of fresh pork meat remaining.

This bounty of pork was celebrated with feasting, with every part of the pig being used. In the canton of Fribourg today, the timing of the Bénichon celebration also coincides with the annual harvest and the time of year for slaughtering pigs. Family and friends gather to enjoy time-honored dishes, such as ham, smoked bacon and sausages.

A friend who grew up near Romont (Fribourg) in the 1950s told me she remembered eating pork so often one year that she and her sister were getting tired of it. When they saw the butcher's truck coming up the road with their delivery, they were sure he was bringing some chicken. Instead, he brought a pig's head and her sister cried in disappointment. The family laughs about it now, but at the time, she was quite upset!

More traditional recipes for Fricassée Genevoise add pig's blood to the red wine sauce just before serving, while more modern versions skip this ingredient altogether. The red wine marinade used to braise the meat still tastes very good without it.

㉒ STUNGGIS

PORK & CABBAGE STEW

You will find this pork and cabbage stew in central Switzerland. I brightened it up with the addition of some apple cider vinegar. Double this recipe if you are feeding a crowd or would like to have leftovers for another meal.

Servings: 4

Prep: 40–45 mins
Cook: about 1 ¾ hours

INGREDIENTS:

1 tablespoon unsalted butter

400 g stewing pork, cut into 5 cm (2 in) chunks (¾ lb)

1 large onion, finely chopped (1 cup)

1 leek, halved and sliced (white and green parts) (1 ½–2 cups)

1 clove garlic, minced

3 tablespoons apple cider vinegar

2 carrots, sliced into 2.5 cm (1 in) pieces (2 cups)

½ celery root, diced (2–3 cups)

½ teaspoon marjoram

½ teaspoon thyme

1 pinch nutmeg

1 liter vegetable stock (p. 19) (4 ¼ cups)

1 large potato, peeled and diced (1 cup)

1 large handful savoy cabbage, chopped

TO GARNISH:

fresh parsley, finely chopped

green onions, finely sliced

INSTRUCTIONS:

1. Melt the butter in a large pot over medium-high heat. Then add the pork chunks, stirring occasionally for 5–10 minutes. When the meat has browned on all sides, remove it from the pot.

2. Reduce the heat to medium. Add the onion, leek and garlic to the same pot and cook for 5–10 minutes, stirring frequently, until the onion becomes translucent. Add the vinegar to the pot and scrape up any brown bits that have stuck to the bottom. Next, stir in the carrot, celery root, marjoram, thyme and nutmeg. Cook for a few more minutes, stirring frequently.

3. Add the meat back to the pot, stir in the vegetable stock and bring to a boil. Reduce the heat to a simmer, cover the pot and let it cook for 1 hour, stirring occasionally.

4. Take the lid off the pot and add the potato and cabbage. Increase the heat to bring it to a boil again, then reduce to a rapid simmer. Let everything cook together for about 30 minutes until the potatoes and cabbage are tender. Stir in the fresh parsley and garnish with finely sliced green onions.

A "MASHED" STEW, IN NAME ONLY, FROM CENTRAL SWITZERLAND

CENTRAL SWITZERLAND

A meat stew found in central Switzerland takes its name from a Swiss German word, *stungge*, that means something like to crush, to push or to stuff. However, this does not relate to the way the dish known as Stunggis is actually prepared today! In Nidwalden and neighboring Obwalden, you add potatoes to Stunggis, but they never get mashed—unless you do it yourself at the table. Ideal for colder weather, this dish also routinely contains cabbage and carrots. Other vegetables added to the stew vary from recipe to recipe. They can include green beans, leeks or kohlrabi.

Sometimes this dish is called Unterwaldner Stunggis, with a historical place name for both the cantons of Obwalden and Nidwalden, who have historically been at odds. Apparently, each of these cantons have wanted to claim Stunggis as their own at one time or another, like with the legend surrounding the Obwaldeners' recipe for Hindersi-Magronen (p.107). It seems that Nidwaldner Stunggis has become the more common name for this dish today, at least according to my Internet searches. Obwalden may have kept their secret macaroni recipe safe, but it seems Nidwalden may have succeeded in declaring Stunggis as its own.

The word *Stunggis* is found in other Swiss dishes as well. For example, the Swiss dish Birestunggis contains a mixture of mashed potatoes and pears. I also saw a 1946 reference to an Obwaldner Zigerstunggis containing Ziger (a fresh cheese made from whey), butter, flour and sugar in the *Schweizerisches Idiotikon*, a lexicon of the Swiss German language.

Unterwaldner Stunggis recipes generally call for beef or pork, but I have most often seen them with pork. I added a few tablespoons of apple cider vinegar to my recipe to give the broth a gentle sour kick. It reminds me of a lighter version of the heavy beef stews I ate growing up in the US but with vegetables that still retain some texture.

OSSO BUCO

BRAISED PORK SHANKS

Although Osso Buco is usually made from veal, I had a version with pork shanks at Osteria Manciana in Ticino's Muggio Valley. This restaurant's version is the inspiration for this recipe. When served with polenta, this dish makes for an extra special weekend supper.

Servings: 4

Prep: about 30 mins
Cook: about 2 hours

INGREDIENTS:

1 tablespoon olive oil

4 pork shanks
(about 750 g / 1 2/3 lbs)

½ teaspoon salt

1 large onion, finely chopped
(1 cup)

2 cloves garlic, minced

2 carrots, finely chopped (1 cup)

1 teaspoon dried oregano

2 sprigs fresh thyme
(or 1 teaspoon dried)

2 bay leaves

120 ml red wine (½ cup)

280 g canned diced tomatoes
(9 oz)

60 ml water (¼ cup)

salt and pepper, to taste

Piment d'Espelette or cayenne
pepper, to taste

1 tablespoon balsamic vinegar

TO GARNISH:

fresh parsley, finely chopped

zest of 1 lemon (optional)

SERVING SUGGESTIONS:

polenta or mashed potatoes

INSTRUCTIONS:

1. Add the olive oil to a large pot over medium-high heat. Sprinkle the pork shanks with the salt and add them to the pot. Brown the meat on all sides, then take it out of the pot and transfer to a plate.

2. To the same pot, add the onion and lower the heat to medium. Cook for about 5 minutes, stirring occasionally, until it becomes translucent. Then stir in the garlic, carrots, oregano, thyme and bay leaves and cook for a few minutes more, stirring frequently.

3. Add the pork shanks back to the pot. Pour in the red wine and scrape up any brown bits from the bottom. Next, stir in the tomatoes and water. Sprinkle with pepper and piment d'Espelette. Cover the pot and bring the mixture to a boil. Then reduce the heat and simmer for about 1 ½ hours or until the meat falls off the bone.

4. When the pork is ready, remove the sprigs of thyme and the bay leaves and discard. Take about half of the broth out of the pot and blend it until smooth with an upright or immersion blender. Add the blended broth back to the pan and stir in the balsamic vinegar. Let the sauce simmer for about 5 minutes more and then serve the pork shanks with the sauce on a bed of polenta or mashed potatoes. Garnish with some fresh parsley and lemon zest (optional).

BRAISED PORK SHANKS WITH RED POLENTA AT THE SMUGGLER'S INN

CANTON TICINO

You feel the history when you visit Ticino's Valle di Muggio. I travelled on narrow roads hugging the hillside through this remote valley to visit two important culinary destinations.

My first destination was Scudellate, located 904 meters (about 3,000 feet) above sea level at the valley's end. Given its proximity to the Italian border, this location has over the years served as a stop for soldiers, border guards, tourists, seasonal workers and others, including smugglers carrying contraband in the 1960s. I arrived just before midday and received a warm greeting at the door of the Osteria Manciana. For nearly a century, the Piffaretti family has been managing this small inn and restaurant that serves regional specialties.

For lunch, I had the Osso Buco with polenta, a signature dish at the Osteria. The tender, slow-cooked pork shank was nestled in a bed of stone-ground polenta made from an heirloom variety of red corn. Sitting next to the fireplace, I sipped on a glass of Ticinese Merlot. Today, this cozy inn is part of an

Albergo Diffuso, a collection of overnight accommodation around Mount Generoso, including a youth hostel also located in Scudellate.

After this satisfying meal, I headed on to my next destination, Il Mulino di Bruzella, the mill that ground the polenta. I hiked down from the nearby village of Cabbio in the autumn sunshine to the cool, dampness of the shady valley floor, cut through by the Breggia river—the mill's source of power. A mill has stood at this site along an old mule path since the 13th century.

The mill facilities are now managed by the Museo etnografico della Valle di Muggio (Ethnographic Museum of the Muggio Valley) and are open to the public. The mill grinds the whole kernels of both red and yellow corn into fine flour and coarse polenta. When you buy some at the mill to cook at home, you get a taste of the history of this incredibly scenic valley.

JACQUERIE NEUCHÂTELOISE REVISITÉE

CHICKEN & SAUERKRAUT WITH BOILED POTATOES

This recipe from the canton of Neuchâtel traditionally calls for snails nested in sauerkraut. I chose instead to follow the more modern adaptation of this dish, which replaces the snails with chicken. Serve it with peeled boiled potatoes.

Servings: 4

Prep: 15–30 mins
Cook: about 1 hour

INGREDIENTS:

SAUERKRAUT:

1 tablespoon unsalted butter

1 medium onion, finely chopped (½ cup)

500 g raw sauerkraut (18 oz)

½ teaspoon juniper berries

½ teaspoon caraway seeds

240 ml dry white wine (e.g., Chasselas or Sauvignon Blanc) (1 cup)

CHICKEN:

1 tablespoon unsalted butter or olive oil

300 g chicken breast, chopped into 2–3 cm (1 in) pieces (⅔ lb)

½ teaspoon salt

SAUCE:

2 tablespoons unsalted butter

1 shallot, finely chopped

1 clove garlic, minced

2 tablespoons all-purpose flour

120 ml dry white wine (½ cup)

120 ml vegetable stock (p. 19) (½ cup)

1–2 tablespoons light cream

1 tablespoon fresh parsley, finely chopped

salt and pepper, to taste

SERVING SUGGESTIONS:

peeled boiled potatoes

INSTRUCTIONS:

1. **Prepare the sauerkraut.** Melt the butter in a large frying pan over medium heat. Add the onion and cook for about 5 minutes until it becomes translucent. Stir in the sauerkraut, juniper berries and caraway seeds. Then add the white wine. Cover and cook over medium heat for 45 minutes. When the sauerkraut has about 30 minutes left to cook, start preparing the chicken.

2. **Brown the chicken.** Heat the butter in another large frying pan over medium-high heat. Sprinkle the chicken with salt and place it in the pan. Cook the chicken, stirring frequently, until it has browned, but is not fully cooked. Transfer the chicken to a plate and cover to keep it warm.

3. **Prepare the sauce.** To the same frying pan you used for the chicken, reduce the heat to medium and add the butter, shallot and garlic. Cook for a few minutes and then whisk in the

flour until well combined. After that, whisk in the wine and vegetable stock to make a smooth broth. Add the chicken back to the pan and bring the mixture to a boil. Reduce the heat, cover the pan and let it simmer for 10–15 minutes until the sauce has thickened and the chicken is fully cooked. Stir in the cream and parsley.

4. **Plate the dish.** When the sauerkraut and the chicken are both done, add a bed of sauerkraut to a plate (removing the juniper berries) and top with some of the chicken and the sauce. Serve immediately with peeled boiled potatoes.

SAUERKRAUT AND SNAILS FROM A NEUCHÂTEL MONASTERY?

CANTON NEUCHÂTEL

Like a stereotypical American, I must confess that I have shied away from eating snails. In the canton of Neuchâtel, where I live, there is a traditional dish known as Jacquerie Neuchâteloise that features snails nestled in a bed of *choucroute* (sauerkraut). You place a dollop of herbed butter and crème fraiche on top before placing everything under the broiler. From my experience, awareness of this dish in the canton and the frequency in which people eat it nowadays is rather low.

In *Neuchâtel à Table* (Neuchâtel to the Table, 1973), the authors, Marcel North and Jacques Montandon, describe how they think Jacquerie Neuchâteloise got its name. They believe a local doctor dined at the monastery in Hauterive long ago and tasted this renowned dish made by the monks. He got permission from them to share it with others, and his name, Jacques, became connected with the dish.

Chef René Merlotti has been credited with inventing the modern recipe for Jacquerie Neuchâteloise in the 20th century.

He worked at several well-known establishments in the city of Neuchâtel, such as the Beau-Rivage Hotel and the Hôtel DuPeyrou. You can still find this dish from time to time on restaurant menus in the canton.

I prefer to make Jacquerie Neuchâteloise with chicken, hence the *revisitée* (revisited) in the name. A number of recipes online also replace the snails with chicken. These recipes call for a sauce made with ingredients such as egg yolk, white wine, Worcestershire sauce and anchovies, among other ingredients.

If you like snails, I encourage you to try this dish at a restaurant in Neuchâtel, but if you are like me, you can enjoy my chicken version at home. The tangy sauerkraut tastes delicious with the tender chicken and boiled potatoes.

30 RIZ CASIMIR

CHICKEN CURRY WITH FRUIT

A retro dish that originated in German-speaking Switzerland, Riz Casimir is served with fruit such as pineapple, bananas and cherries. I owe some of the variations in my recipe to my friend Maria. She grew up in India but has called Switzerland her home since 2006.

Servings: 4

Prep: 20–30 mins
Cook: 35–45 mins

INGREDIENTS:

1 tablespoon canola or vegetable oil

1 large onion, finely chopped (1 cup)

1 thumb–sized knob of fresh ginger, peeled and finely grated or chopped

1 clove garlic, minced

1 medium tomato, diced (½ cup)

3 tablespoons curry powder

1 teaspoon salt

4 chicken breasts, cut into 2–3 cm (1 in) pieces

1 red bell pepper, chopped

1 tablespoon all-purpose flour

300 ml water (1 ¼ cups)

120 ml light cream (½ cup)

TO GARNISH:

fresh apple slices

fresh sliced pineapple or canned pineapple rings

dried banana chips

toasted almonds

fresh cilantro, chopped

SERVING SUGGESTIONS:

basmati rice

INSTRUCTIONS:

1. Heat the oil in a large pan over medium heat. Sauté the onion for about 5 minutes or until it becomes translucent. Then add the ginger and garlic and cook for 1 minute. Next, add the tomato and cook for 2–3 minutes more, stirring frequently. Finally, stir in the curry powder and salt. Continue cooking on a medium-low heat for 8–10 minutes.

2. Add the chicken and red pepper to the pan. In a small bowl, whisk the flour into the water. Add this to the pan, increase the heat to medium-high and bring the mixture to a low boil. Then, lower the heat to medium, cover the pan and simmer for 15–20 minutes until the chicken is fully cooked.

3. Remove the lid and stir in the light cream until it has heated through and the sauce has thickened slightly.

4. Serve immediately with rice. Garnish with fresh apple slices, pineapple, banana chips, toasted almonds and fresh cilantro.

A SWISS RETRO CURRY WITH COLORFUL FRUIT

SUISSE ALÉMANIQUED

I once posted a photo on Instagram of my homemade Riz Casimir. It showed a ring of rice with a Swiss version of a chicken curry nestled inside. Around the rice, were half circles of canned pineapple rings and canned cherries. Over the curry, I had sprinkled toasted flaked almonds. My question posed in the caption was "Should this be part of Switzerland's culinary heritage?"

The founder of Mövenpick restaurants, Ueli Prager, introduced Riz Casimir to Switzerland in 1952. The dish had ingredients considered exotic at that time in Switzerland, such as curry, pineapple and banana. Prager's original recipe called for veal. He cooked the fruit in the curry, but some recipes call for it on the side. Sometimes, it also has a savory whipped cream on top. Full of color, this super-easy and kid–friendly dish has great textures and a blend of sweet and savory flavors. Mr. Prager created a hit.

Although, not everyone is a fan. Over the years, I have heard snickers from the French-speaking Swiss when I mention this dish. They poke fun at their German-speaking compatriots' fondness for combining fruity flavors with savory dishes (e.g., Hindersi-Magronen; macaroni and cheese with applesauce, p. 107). Switzerland's retro curry also made headlines in 2023 when the online food directory, Taste Atlas, declared it to be one of the top 20 worst dishes in the world.

Numerous people who grew up eating this dish love it and continue to make it at home. Someone wrote in reply to my Instagram post, "My absolute favorite. This dish is definitely part of my life! Great memories [of] going to Mövenpick as a child with my family and introducing it to my kids."

My version of Riz Casimir includes chopped tomato and allows plenty of time to cook it with the curry powder, which are both inspired by a recipe from my friend Maria de Conceicao, a food photographer and stylist. Born in India, she moved to Switzerland to work for a radio station in Zurich. The first time she tried Riz Casimir she thought, "Wait a minute. This is not a curry!" The name of the dish threw her off, as she thought it referred to a Kashmiri-style curry. Over time though, the dish has grown on her. She likes the combination of fruit and curry, a pairing she already knows from Indian mango curries.

31

GESCHNETZELTES MIT PILZEN
SLICED BEEF & MUSHROOMS

This well-known Swiss dish is typically paired with Rösti (p. 81), but you can also serve it with egg noodles or rice. The original recipe is made with veal, but I typically make it with beef because it is generally cheaper and easier to find.

Servings: 4

Prep: 20–30 mins
Cook: 20–30 mins

INGREDIENTS:

500 g beef tenderloin, sliced into thin strips (1 lb)

½ teaspoon salt

2 tablespoons all-purpose flour

2 tablespoons unsalted butter

1 medium onion, finely chopped (½ cup)

1 clove garlic, minced

120 ml dry white wine (or vegetable stock, p. 19) (½ cup)

1 tablespoon Worcestershire sauce

300 g fresh mixed mushrooms (e.g., brown, Shitake, oyster), sliced (10 oz)

240 ml vegetable stock, (p. 19) (1 cup)

60 ml light cream (¼ cup)

1 tablespoon cognac (optional)

salt and freshly ground black pepper, to taste

TO GARNISH:

1 handful parsley, finely chopped

SERVING SUGGESTIONS:

Rösti (p. 81), mashed potatoes, egg noodles or rice

INSTRUCTIONS:

1. Add the thinly sliced beef to a medium bowl and sprinkle with the salt. Then add the flour and toss the beef to coat it evenly.

2. Heat 1 tablespoon of the butter in a large frying pan over medium-high heat. Add the beef to the pan and sear on all sides until just browned, turning frequently. Transfer the meat to a bowl and cover it to keep the meat warm.

3. Reduce the heat to medium and add the second tablespoon of butter, followed by the onion and garlic. Cook for about 5 minutes, stirring frequently, until the onion becomes translucent.

4. Then, add the white wine and Worcestershire sauce to the same pan to deglaze it, scraping any browned bits from the bottom. When the wine has reduced by half (3–5 minutes), add the mushrooms to the pan and sauté until they soften (about 5 minutes).

5. Return the beef to the pan. Stir everything together until the meat is evenly distributed in the mushroom mixture. Pour in the vegetable stock and simmer for 3–5 minutes, just until the meat is fully cooked.

6. Stir in the cream and cognac until it is heated through. Season with salt and pepper. Serve with Rösti (p. 81), egg noodles or rice. Garnish with parsley.

Variation:
For a vegetarian version of this dish, omit the beef and increase the amount of mushrooms to 800 grams. Start making this recipe at Step 3.

ZURICH'S MOST FAMOUS DISH

CANTON ZURICH

Zürcher Geschnetzeltes (sliced meat Zurich style; known as *Züri Gschnätzlets* in Swiss German) is often prepared with veal and mushrooms, served in a light brown sauce made from cream and white wine, and with a side of Rösti (p. 81). A Swiss journalist once contacted me for my opinion on where to find the best version of this dish. The restaurant I ultimately recommended was a bit unorthodox. One of my favorite interpretations of this famous Swiss dish is from Hiltl, the oldest vegetarian restaurant in the world. They make it with organic seitan instead of veal.

Numerous other restaurants in Zurich have *Geschnetzeltes* on the menu, with one of the most well-known prepared by Restaurant Kronenhalle. Opened in 1924, the dining rooms of this restaurant are decorated with world-class artworks from Pablo Picasso, Joan Miró and Marc Chagall. Unlike most recipes, this restaurant purees the mushrooms in its sauce.

An early recipe for Kalbsgeschnetzeltes (sliced veal) comes from Marie Imhoof's 1903 *Schweizerisches Familien Kochbuch* (Swiss Family Cookbook). However, the origin of this dish is more often linked to a 1947 cookbook by Rosa Graf. Entitled *Goldene Kochfibel* (Golden Cooking Primer), this more than 750-page tome includes a very basic description of *Geschnetzeltes Kalbfleisch*. It appears under the heading "À la minute," dishes cooked just before serving. "The less the meat is roasted, the more tender it remains," she advises. There are no mushrooms in her recipe, which are standard today, nor kidneys, which were added over the years but now are rarely seen in restaurants. This dish was first connected with Zurich in the 1948 cookbook, *Das Neue Kochbuch* (The New Cookbook) by Willy Brenneisen.

Regional variations also exist for this dish. At the Bürgenstock Resort above Lake Lucerne, I had Nidwaldner *Geschnetzeltes* served with sliced grapes. Basel's version uses tomato puree, paprika and beer. At Jack's Brasserie in Bern's Hotel Schweizerhof, the Geschnetzeltes arrives at your table in a little cast iron pot. They serve you a portion with crisp Rösti and then keep the pot warm over a burner nearby—a lovely way to serve this dish.

32 OMELETTEN UND GHACKETS
CRÊPES & SAUCY GROUND BEEF

These savory Swiss German-style crêpes have a ground beef filling that is especially popular with children. Vegetarian fillings also work well with Omeletten. Or, you could serve a generous spoonful of Ghackets with macaroni and applesauce, another very Swiss German dish.

Servings: 4 (8–10 Omeletten)

Prep: 40–45 mins
Cook: 30–40 mins

INGREDIENTS:

OMELETTEN:

350 g all-purpose flour
(2 ¾ cups)

½ teaspoon salt

4 large eggs

240 ml water (1 cup)

240 ml milk (1 cup)

1–2 teaspoons unsalted butter

GHACKETS:

450 g ground beef (1 lb)

1 medium onion, finely chopped
(½ cup)

1 clove garlic, minced

1 carrot, very finely chopped
(½ cup)

1 celery stalk, very finely chopped
(½ cup)

80 ml red wine (or vegetable
stock, p. 19) (⅓ cup)

360 ml tomato puree or passata
(1 ½ cups)

1 bay leaf

1–2 sprigs fresh thyme
(or ½ teaspoon dried thyme)

fresh parsley, finely chopped

salt and pepper, to taste

INSTRUCTIONS:

1. **Prepare the batter for the Omeletten.** Add the flour and salt to a large bowl and whisk together. Make a well in the center and add the eggs, water and milk. Whisk together until the batter becomes smooth and well combined. Let the batter rest at room temperature for 30 minutes.

2. **Make the Ghackets.** Add the ground beef to a large frying pan over medium-high heat and cook until browned. Then tilt the pan to spoon out some of the excess fat into a heat-safe bowl. Let the fat cool slightly before discarding.

3. Add the onion, garlic, carrot and celery to the pan. Sauté for about 5 minutes, stirring occasionally, until the onion becomes translucent. Next, add the red wine, tomato puree, bay leaf and thyme. Simmer over medium heat for about 20 minutes. While the meat is simmering, cook the Omeletten.

4. **Cook the Omeletten.** Melt the butter in a special crepe pan or other small frying pan over medium-high heat. Using a ladle, pour in some of the batter. Tilt the pan around as needed to make sure the batter spreads evenly across the pan to form a thin, round layer. Cook for a few minutes on each side until lightly browned.

5. Stir the chopped parsley into the meat mixture, then add 2–3 large spoonfuls to each Omelette, roll it up and serve immediately.

Make-ahead tips:
Prepare the batter in the morning and store in the refrigerator until you need it in the evening.

You can also make the Ghackets in advance. After cooking, let it cool and refrigerate for 1–2 days until you need it. If the Ghackets mixture is too thick when you reheat it, you can add some more tomato puree or passata.

CRÊPE-LIKE OMELETTEN WITH A SAVORY FILLING

SUISSE ALÉMANIQUED

Switzerland has different types of omelets, depending on which linguistic region you are in. The one important difference between them? Flour.

In French-speaking Switzerland, eggs will be the primary ingredient in your omelet. It will probably not contain any flour and will resemble an *omelette* across the border in France. In German-speaking Switzerland, however, Omeletten are generally made with flour. As a result, they look and taste more like a thicker version of crêpes.

One classic Swiss German filling for Omeletten is made with ground beef and vegetables and reminds me of a Bolognese sauce. It goes by the name *Ghackets*, which literally means "ground" or "minced" meat. You also find this sauce paired with Hörnli (the Swiss German term for elbow macaroni), a variation you can easily make using the Ghackets part of my recipe. This savory dish is usually served with applesauce, similar to Hindersi-Magronen (p. 107).

Of course, Omeletten also work well with other types of fillings. For a sweet version, you could fill them with poached apples or your favorite jam. For a vegetarian version, you could fill them with sautéed spinach and mushrooms. Or you could use a mixture of sautéed onions, grated sweet potato and cayenne pepper, sprinkled with fresh cilantro and cheese. Once again, this is another recipe you can adapt to your taste.

Whatever pairing you choose for the Omeletten or the Ghackets, the dish will be the perfect comfort food for a weeknight meal.

HACKTÄTSCHLI

BREADED MEAT PATTIES

Before frying these little ground beef patties, you coat them in breadcrumbs. This gives them a little more texture and helps you use up stale bread at the same time. Serve with your favorite condiments.

Servings: 4 (about 15 patties)

Prep: 20–30 mins
Cook: 15–20 mins

INGREDIENTS:

MEAT PATTIES:

300 g ground beef (10 oz)

80 ml milk (⅓ cup)

1 large egg

1 medium onion, finely chopped (½ cup)

half a carrot, grated (¼ cup)

1 garlic clove, minced

2 tablespoons rolled oats

2 tablespoons breadcrumbs (p. 17)

1 small handful fresh parsley, finely chopped

1 teaspoon, dried tarragon

½ teaspoon salt

freshly ground pepper, to taste

BREADCRUMB COATING:

50 g breadcrumbs (½ cup) (p. 17)

½ teaspoon paprika

FOR FRYING:

2 tablespoons unsalted butter

SERVING SUGGESTIONS:

Creamy Lemon Herb Sauce (p. 162), roasted tomato sauce or your favorite condiments.

INSTRUCTIONS:

1. Add all the ingredients for the meat patties to a large bowl and mix everything together until well combined. Form about 15 small patties with a diameter of about 5 cm (2 in). Set aside.

2. Prepare the breadcrumb coating in a shallow bowl by whisking together the breadcrumbs and paprika. Coat each of the patties on all sides in this mixture.

3. Preheat the oven to 150°C (300°F). In a frying pan over medium-high heat, melt 1 tablespoon of butter and cook half of the patties for 5–7 minutes on each side until browned. After that, put them on a baking sheet lined with parchment paper and place them in the oven for about 5–10 minutes to finish cooking. Then add the other tablespoon of butter to the pan and cook the remaining patties, repeating the process. Serve immediately.

CREAMY LEMON HERB SAUCE

Serve this sauce with the Hacktätschli (p. 161) or with boiled potatoes and Stupfete (p. 93).

Servings: 4

Prep: 5 minutes

INGREDIENTS:

200 g crème fraiche or sour cream
(generous 1 cup)

1 small handful of fresh herbs
(e.g., parsley or chives)

2 tablespoons lemon juice, freshly
squeezed

1 clove garlic, minced

salt and pepper, to taste

INSTRUCTIONS:

Mix all the ingredients together until well-combined. Refrigerate the sauce until you are ready to use it. It is best served the same day.

A SWISS LINK TO THE ORIGIN OF MEATBALLS?

SUISSE ALÉMANIQUED

You could say that the origin of meatballs has a Swiss connection. An early recipe for meatballs comes from Maestro Martino, who was born in Ticino in the late Middle Ages. He has been described as the world's first celebrity chef because he left the village of Grumo in the Blenio Valley to become the favored chef of elite families in Milan and two popes in Rome. His cookbook, *Libro de Arte Coquinaria* (Book on the Art of Cooking), published in the second half of the 15th century, includes a recipe for *polpetta*. Although the *polpetta* described in this recipe resembles a roll more than a sphere, it was an early use of the term that today means meatball in Italian.

Hacktätschli, a comfort food recipe found in Switzerland's German-speaking regions, feels both old school and modern at the same time. I sometimes struggle to keep my meatballs perfectly round and browned on all sides, so I love this recipe because I can flatten the meatballs into patties instead.

I developed my recipe for Hacktätschli years ago, inspired by a recipe from the canton of Uri that I found in a little cookbook, *Les recettes des Grand-Mère*,

Tome 4 (Grandma's Recipes, Volume 4, 2011), that I picked up at a second-hand shop. The recipe coats the meat patties in breadcrumbs before frying them, giving them a slightly crunchy outer texture. Since that time, I have seen numerous other Swiss German recipes developed by Michelin-starred chefs and food critics, among others that use this same technique.

In general, Hacktätschli are a great way to stretch your meat budget and use up stale bread. You can also add leftover vegetables to the meat mixture. For my recipe, I throw in half a grated carrot, but you could add leftover steamed broccoli or roasted cauliflower instead. These old methods to extend limited resources and reduce waste still make sense today.

34 STEAK VIGNERON

WINEGROWER'S HAMBURGER STEAK SANDWICH

Upgrade your hamburger with this seasoned patty recipe from the canton of Neuchâtel. You can keep it simple and just serve it on a bread roll (p. 166) or you can add your favorite hamburger toppings. I also enjoy cooking these on the grill in summer.

Servings: 6 (makes 6 patties)

Prep: 20–30 mins
Cook: 10–15 mins

INGREDIENTS:

450–500 g ground beef
(about 1 lb)

50 g breadcrumbs (p. 17) (½ cup)

60 ml dry red wine (or milk)
(¼ cup)

1 large egg

1 shallot or small onion, minced
(about ⅓ cup)

1 clove garlic, minced

1 teaspoon salt

½ teaspoon ground white pepper

½ teaspoon dried oregano

½ teaspoon dried thyme

1 pinch cayenne pepper

FOR FRYING:

1–2 tablespoons unsalted butter

SERVING SUGGESTION:

Bread rolls (p. 166) and your
favorite toppings

INSTRUCTIONS:

1. In a large bowl, mix all the ingredients together with your hands until well combined. Form the mixture into 6 rectangular patties about 7 x 10 cm (3 x 4 in).

2. Melt the butter in a large frying pan over medium-high heat. Fry the patties on both sides (all at once or in batches) until they are cooked to your liking. Alternatively, you can cook them on the grill. Place on a buttered bun and serve immediately.

    Make-ahead tip: Make the patties in the morning, cover and refrigerate until you are ready to cook them in the evening.

PETITS PAINS MAISON

HOMEMADE BREAD ROLLS

These are easy homemade bread rolls to serve with Steak Vigneron (p. 165) or to accompany any of the soups in Chapter III or the other meat dishes in this chapter.

Servings: 8 rolls

Prep: about 3 ½ hours
Bake: 20–30 mins

INGREDIENTS:

20 g fresh yeast, crumbled, or 8 g active dry yeast (2 ¼ teaspoons)

300 ml water, lukewarm
(1 ¼ cups)

500 g bread or all-purpose flour
(4 cups)

1 ½ teaspoons salt

SPRINKLE ON BEFORE BAKING:

1 tablespoon all-purpose flour

INSTRUCTIONS:

1. In a small bowl, add the yeast to the lukewarm water. Let it sit for a few minutes and then whisk together until the yeast has fully dissolved.

2. Whisk the flour and salt together in a large bowl. Make a well in the center. Pour the yeast mixture into the well. Stir everything together until a dough forms. Then, knead the dough for about 10 minutes by hand or use an electric mixer with a dough hook. When the dough becomes smooth and elastic, place it in a bowl covered with a damp kitchen towel for 1–2 hours at room temperature or until it doubles in size.

3. Separate the dough into 8 pieces. Shape each of the pieces into elongated oval buns about 7 x 11 cm (about 3 x 4 in). Place the buns on a baking sheet lined with parchment paper. Using the tablespoon of flour, lightly dust the surface of the buns and cover them with a dry kitchen towel. Let them rest at room temperature for about 1 hour.

4. Bake the buns for 20–30 minutes at 200°C (400°F) until they become lightly browned. Cool completely on a wire rack. Serve the same day they are baked for maximum taste and freshness.

A POPULAR SANDWICH AT NEUCHÂTEL'S FÊTE DES VENDANGES

CANTON NEUCHÂTEL

The Fête des Vendanges, celebrating Neuchâtel's wine harvest, starts Friday afternoon with an *apéro* and does not really stop until late Sunday night—immediately followed by the noise of cleaning crews. I first encountered Steak Vigneron at this raucous event. According to our local newspaper, these seasoned meat patty sandwiches started appearing at the fête in the late 1970s. They have remained a staple culinary offering at local fêtes and festivals in Neuchâtel like this one, especially in the fall.

Almost always prepared by butchers rather than at home, the type of meat used in the Steak Vigneron varies. Butchers sometimes mix beef with pork or also horsemeat. When I first moved to Switzerland, this shocked me because no one eats horsemeat in the US. I once attended a press conference held at a butcher shop in the canton of Jura and watched as the butcher fed the horsemeat into the grinder. I sampled horsemeat salami, a bit reluctantly, and have not had any since.

In December 2019, a few years after my visit to the butcher shop, the Association Patrimoine Culinaire Suisse (Culinary Heritage of Switzerland Association) added horsemeat to its inventory of traditional Swiss food products. In the press release, they stated that 90% of the horsemeat consumed in Switzerland is imported. Furthermore, it placed per capita consumption at around 450 grams per year. Recent data indicates a downward trend. Proviande, the Swiss inter-professional association for the meat industry, estimates the 2022 per capita consumption at only 240 grams—a small amount compared to 20.7 kilograms for pork during the same year.

When I make Steak Vigneron at home, I prefer to use 100% beef. I also add a splash of red wine to the patty mix to honor the name of the dish, but apparently this is not always done. My favorite way to enjoy these sandwiches is with a soft, floury bun (p. 166) and a smear of mayonnaise.

SAVORY TARTS & BAKES

I love baking, so you can imagine that this is one of my favorite chapters in the book. These 10 recipes are all baked in the oven, with a few also requiring a bit of cooking on the stove beforehand. Some of these recipes take a bit of effort, but you can often tackle a step or two in advance, such as making the pastry. And, when you finally put everything in the oven, you have the gift of time to either clean up or prepare a salad.

To start, there are recipes for eight savory tarts from across Switzerland. I begin with a recipe for Rüebli-Quiche (carrot quiche) with goat cheese and dill (p. 171), inspired by my visit to the annual carrot market in Aarau. The tour of tarts continues with stops in the Jura, Schaffhausen, Fribourg, Graubünden (for two tarts), Bern and Ticino!

Half of the recipes in this chapter are vegetarian. I also provide vegetarian alternatives when possible. Of the recipes with meat, three contain bacon: Bölletünne (onion tart, p. 179), Speckkuchen (bacon flatbread, p. 191) and Gâteau Saviésan (potato, leek and cheese pie, p. 183). The other two recipes contain either ground beef, Churer Fleischtorte (Chur meat pie, p. 187), or ground pork, Wurstweggen (sausage rolls, p. 207).

The final two recipes, while baked, are not tarts. The first is Käseschnitte (p. 203), an open-faced grilled cheese sandwich and one of the easiest and quickest recipes in this book! The second is the versatile Wurstweggen (p. 207) which I make with a filling of ground pork, grated apple and fennel seeds.

I predict that a recipe in this chapter will become one of your best-loved supper dishes, which you will make time and again.

35 RÜEBLI-QUICHE

CARROT QUICHE

A slice of carrot quiche from the famous Rüeblimärt (carrot market) in Aarau inspired this recipe. I like the combination of the sweet carrots with the tangy goat cheese and fresh dill. This tart tastes good any time of day—for breakfast, lunch or supper!

Servings: 6

Prep: about 1 ½ hours
(incl. time for the dough to chill)
Bake: 35–40 mins

INGREDIENTS:

PASTRY:

200 g all-purpose flour (1 ⅔ cups)

¼ teaspoon salt

freshly ground pepper, to taste

100 g unsalted butter, cold
(scant ½ cup)

4–5 tablespoons water, cold

FILLING:

1 tablespoon all-purpose flour

60 ml light cream (¼ cup)

½ teaspoon salt

freshly ground black pepper, to taste

5 large eggs

85 g goat cheese, crumbled
(about 3 oz)

2 carrots, cooked* and finely chopped (1 cup)

1 small handful fresh dill, finely chopped

*You can roast carrots for this recipe (see make-ahead tips, p. 172) or use leftover cooked carrots.

INSTRUCTIONS:

1. **Prepare the pastry dough.** Whisk the flour, salt and pepper together in a large bowl. Add the cold butter in pieces. Use a pastry blender or two knives to cut the butter pieces into the flour mixture until they become the size of small pebbles. Make a well in the center and add the cold water. Stir everything together just until a smooth dough forms. Shape the dough into a disk, wrap it in parchment paper and refrigerate for 30–60 minutes until chilled.

2. Grease a 10 x 35 cm (4 x 14 in) non-stick, rectangular tart pan. You can also use a 28 cm (11 in) round tart pan.

3. Roll out the chilled dough on the sheet of parchment paper to fit the size of the pan. If you are using a non-stick pan, invert the sheet of parchment paper to place the dough in the pan. Otherwise, lay the sheet of parchment paper with the dough onto the pan. Fit the dough into the pan by pressing it into the bottom and sides. Fold over the excess dough on the sides, toward the inside of the tart, to form the outer crust. Prick the bottom of the dough with a fork.

4. **Prepare the filling.** In a large bowl, whisk together the flour, cream, salt and pepper until the mixture is completely smooth. Then beat in the eggs until they are fully incorporated. Onto the dough in the pan, add the crumbled goat cheese, followed by the carrots and then the dill. Pour the egg mixture

over the top. Bake for 35–40 minutes at 200°C (400°F) on the bottom rack of the oven until the pastry has lightly browned and the filling has fully set and become golden.

Make-ahead tips:
Make the dough in the morning and let it sit covered in the refrigerator until you are ready to use it.

Roast the carrots in advance: Peel and slice the carrots in half lengthwise. Add them to a baking sheet lined with parchment paper and drizzle them with some olive oil. Gently toss the carrots to lightly coat them in the oil. Then roast for 30–45 minutes at 200°C (400°F) until they soften. Refrigerate for 2–3 days until you are ready to use them.

A QUICHE INSPIRED BY A SWISS CARROT MARKET

CANTON AARGAU

On the first Wednesday in November, the city of Aarau—the cantonal capital of Aargau—hosts its annual Rüeblimärt (carrot market). The market has over 100 stands with around 60 varieties of carrots for sale, and thousands of visitors. When I arrived one year just after 7:30 a.m., it was already bustling!

Aargau is known for growing carrots. One of its most noteworthy varieties is the Küttiger Rüebli, a special white carrot that has been recognized as part of Switzerland's culinary heritage. Aarau hosted its first Rüeblimärt in 1981 and the tradition has continued ever since. Along with all the colorful carrots, you will find many culinary specialties made with this vegetable, such as sausages, breads, and cakes. The wonderful thing about carrots is that you can use them in both sweet and savory dishes.

Carrots appear everywhere at the market and in creative ways. The first stand I visited had a beautiful sign made from a mosaic of sliced carrots. The fountains had ornamental carrots in flower bouquets and flowerpots. A large heart made from whole carrots surrounded strips of wood hand-painted with the words, "Make Rüeblisuppe [carrot soup], Not War."

At the Rüeblimärt, I found something I had not expected—Rüebli-Quiche. For some reason, it had never occurred to me to add carrots to a quiche and I had to try it. Along with grated carrots, the rich, creamy filling also contained onions. I did some research at a local library and found an Aargauer cookbook with a recipe for a rectangular-shaped carrot quiche with Gruyère cheese.

Back at home, I decided to develop my own recipe, this time combining the carrots with goat cheese and dill. But I preserved the tradition of the rectangular shape that I found in the library cookbook. Who knew that carrots would taste so good in a quiche?

36 GÂTEAU DU CLOÎTRE

CLOISTER TART

This irresistible tart features a bread dough crust filled with cream and cheese. Serve it in thin slices for an apéro or in large slices with soup or a salad for supper.

Servings: 4–6

Prep: about 3 hours
Bake: 20–30 mins

INGREDIENTS:

DOUGH:

10 g fresh yeast, crumbled or 4 g active dry yeast (1 ¼ teaspoon)

125 ml milk, lukewarm (½ cup)

250 g bread or all-purpose flour (2 cups)

½ teaspoon salt

40 g unsalted butter, softened (3 ½ tablespoons)

1 egg white

FILLING:

100 g Tête de Moine cheese, in rosettes or coarsely grated* (3 ½ oz)

200 ml heavy cream (generous ¾ cup)

1 egg yolk

¼ teaspoon salt

TO GARNISH:

fresh chives, finely chopped

*If you can't find Tête de Moine, a specialty from the canton of Jura and the Bernese Jura region, you can use another semi-hard cheese or Gruyère.

INSTRUCTIONS:

1. **Prepare the bread dough.** Add the yeast to the lukewarm milk in a small bowl. Let it sit for a few minutes and then stir until the yeast has completely dissolved.

2. Add the flour and salt to a large bowl. Add the butter in pieces. Make a well in the center and add the yeast mixture and the egg white. Stir everything together until a dough forms. Knead the dough for about 10 minutes by hand on a lightly floured surface, or using an electric mixer with a dough hook, until the dough becomes smooth and elastic.

3. Place the dough back in the large bowl and cover with a damp kitchen towel. Let the dough rise at room temperature for 1–2 hours or until it has doubled in size.

4. When the dough has risen, grease a 25 cm (10 in) round baking pan with butter or line it with parchment paper. Press the dough into the pan, cover and let the dough rise a second time for about 30 minutes.

5. When the dough has completed its second rise, prick the bottom of the dough in several places with a fork. Press the dough up the sides of the pan and create a lip around the edge that will prevent the filling from spilling out. Then add the cheese onto the dough in an even layer, opening up the rosettes of Tête de Moine to completely cover the dough.

6. **Prepare the filling.** In a medium bowl, whisk together the cream, egg yolk and salt. Pour the mixture over the cheese without letting it spill over the edges of the dough.

7. Bake at 200°C (400°F) for 20–30 minutes until the sides and surface of the tart are golden brown and the filling is set. Serve immediately or at room temperature, garnished with fresh chives (if you prefer, sprinkle on the chives before the tart goes in the oven).

Make-ahead tips:
Make the dough in the morning, let it rest on the counter for about 20–30 minutes, and then refrigerate the dough all day in a covered bowl. Take it out of the refrigerator about 1 hour before you plan to use it, so it can warm up. Then continue from step 5 of the recipe.

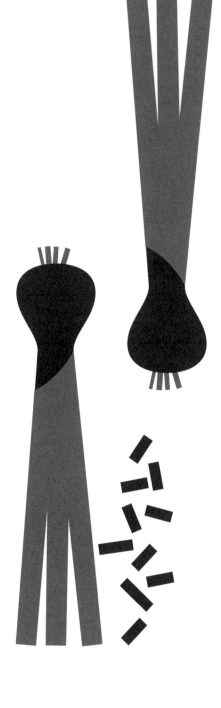

A BREADY TART NAMED FOR ST. URSANNE'S HISTORIC CHURCH

CANTON JURA

I called ahead to reserve my Gâteau du Cloître (cloister cake) at the Yerly bakery in St. Ursanne. Settled in a valley along the river Doubs in the canton of Jura, this quaint medieval village is well worth a visit. And, if you combine your visit with a stop at the bakery where this savory tart was originally created, you have another good reason for the trip.

From the train station in St. Ursanne, I walked downhill and through the Porte Sainte-Pierre, one of three historic gates that serve as points of entry to the village center. After a left turn, I found Boulangerie Yerly, where the yeasted tart with a cream and cheese filling was waiting for me. Under the management of its former owner, Gérard Mahon, the bakery won a gold medal for its Gâteau du Cloître in 2005 at Switzerland's national competition for regional food products, the Concours Suisse des produits du terroir. The Gâteau du Cloître takes its name from the cloister of St. Ursanne's Collégiale (collegiate) church constructed in the 12th and 13th centuries. The cloister, the church's open walkway with arched windows, surrounds a quiet inner courtyard. The Gâteau du Cloître is like a cousin to the

Totché, another yeasted tart from the canton of Jura. While similar to the Totché, the tart from St. Ursanne contains cheese, and specifically Tête de Moine (monk's head), and chopped chives. I have seen similar versions made at other bakeries that go by the name Gâteau des Moines (monks' cake).

Tête de Moine is a semi-hard cheese made with raw cow's milk that comes from the Jura and Bernese Jura regions. To serve it, you scrape thin shavings from the top with a knife—a process simplified by the invention of the girolle in 1982. You stab the middle of the round cheese with the spindle and then swing the blade across the top of the cheese in a circular motion to create perfect rosettes.

There is nothing not to like about the Gâteau du Cloître! And if you make the dough in the morning, you can prepare the tart quickly in the evening with a fresh, crisp salad for a satisfying supper.

37. SCHAFFHAUSER BÖLLETÜNNE

SCHAFFHAUSEN ONION TART

My recipe for Schaffhausen's onion tart includes whole wheat flour in the pastry dough. I have also added a finely chopped red chili for some heat. If you would prefer a vegetarian version of this tart, replace the bacon with a handful of grated cheese such as Gruyère or Emmentaler.

Servings: 6–8

Prep: about 1 hour
(incl. time for the dough to chill)
Bake: 35–45 mins

INGREDIENTS:

DOUGH:

125 g all-purpose flour (1 cup)

75 g whole wheat flour (½ cup)

½ teaspoon salt

85 g unsalted butter, cold
(6 tablespoons)

60 ml water, cold (¼ cup)

FILLING:

50–65 g bacon, finely chopped
(4–6 slices)

250 g onions, finely chopped
(2 cups)

1 red chili pepper, finely chopped
(optional)

1 small handful fresh parsley,
finely chopped

4 large eggs

80 ml light cream (⅓ cup)

80 ml milk (⅓ cup)

1 tablespoon all-purpose flour

½ teaspoon salt

¼ teaspoon freshly ground black
pepper

INSTRUCTIONS:

1. **Prepare the pastry dough.** Whisk the flours together with the salt in a large bowl. Add the cold butter in pieces. Use a pastry blender or two knives to cut the butter pieces into the flour until they become the size of small pebbles. Make a well in the center and add the cold water. Stir everything together to form a dough. Shape the dough into a disk, wrap it in parchment paper and refrigerate for 30–60 minutes. When the dough is nearly done chilling, prepare the filling.

2. **Prepare the filling.** In a large frying pan over medium-high heat, brown the chopped bacon. Drain most of the bacon grease from the pan and reduce the heat to medium. Then add the onions and chili pepper and cook for about 5 minutes until the onions become translucent. Stir in the chopped parsley. Take the pan off the stove and allow the mixture to cool.

3. Grease a 28 cm (11 in) round tart pan. Take the chilled dough out of the refrigerator and roll it out on the parchment paper to fit the bottom and sides of the pan. If you are using a non-stick pan, invert the sheet of parchment paper to place the dough in the pan. Otherwise, lay the sheet of parchment paper with the dough in the pan. Press the dough into the pan and prick the bottom with a fork.

4. Spread the bacon and onion mixture evenly onto the dough. Whisk together the eggs, cream, milk, flour, salt and pepper in a large bowl until the mixture is completely smooth. Then, pour it over the tart.

5. Bake for 30–40 minutes at 200°C (400°F) on the bottom rack until the pastry has lightly browned and the filling has fully set and become golden.

Make-ahead tips:
Make the dough in the morning and leave it in the refrigerator until you are ready to use it in the evening.

SCHAFFHAUSEN'S DISTRACTINGLY GOOD ONION TART

CANTON SCHAFFHAUSEN

A local legend claims that Schaffhausen's Bölletünne, an onion tart, is so good that you can use it to distract your adversaries! The monks at the Klosterinsel Rheinau (Rheinau monastery island) needed money and decided to sell off some land. They put the Rossberg up for auction. The two villages of Hallau and Wilchingen, who did not get along, expressed their interest in acquiring this desirable land. And so the story goes that the Wilchingers distracted the Hallauers with wine and irresistible slices of Bölletünne. This strategy allowed them to score the winning bid at the auction and ultimately secure the land. Today, this forested hill is part of the Schaffhausen Regional Nature Park.

The name Bölletünne combines two words in the local Swiss German dialect: *Bölle* means "onions" and *tünne* comes from the German dünn (thin), referring to the flatness of the onion tart. In Schaffhausen, it is commonly served as an *apéro* with a glass of Federweisser, a local white wine made from Pinot Noir grapes.

Onion tarts are not limited to Schaffhausen, however. You will also find them in Bern and Basel. Bern's *Zwiebelkuchen* (onion cake) is famously served at its *Zibelemärit* (onion market), which takes place every year on the fourth Monday in November. Basel's *Zwiebelwähe* (onion tart) is one of the essential dishes at the annual Fasnacht (carnival) celebrations. All three of these tarts are quite similar, but one distinction is that the Bölletünne nearly always contains bacon, while the tarts in Bern and Basel may or may not.

When I asked the Schaffhauserland Tourism office where to find the Bölletünne in Schaffhausen, they wrote that it is not usually found in restaurants. Instead, they recommended Café-Confiserie Rohr, recognized as one of the 50 most beautiful cafes in Switzerland by the Schweizer Heimatschutz (Swiss Heritage) association. Confiserie Reber also makes the Bölletünne—check out the Schaffhauserzungen sandwich cookies while you are there. For both places, make sure to call ahead because they typically only make the onion tart on Fridays. Due to a Christian tradition, Friday has historically been a meat-free day in Switzerland, when all manner of tarts are commonly served.

38

GÂTEAU SAVIÉSAN

POTATO, LEEK & BACON PIE

This potato and leek pie with bacon and cheese comes from the canton of Valais. I use a homemade short crust pastry in my recipe. Unlike the traditional versions of this pie, I have added a generous sprinkle of poppyseeds for a little extra flavor and texture.

Servings: 6

Prep: about 1 ½ hours
(incl. time for the dough to chill)
Bake: 35–45 mins

INGREDIENTS:

DOUGH:

350 g all-purpose flour
(2 ¾ cups)

1 teaspoon salt

150 g unsalted butter, cold
(⅔ cup)

120 ml water, cold (½ cup)

FILLING:

65 g bacon, chopped
(about 5 slices)

300 g potatoes, peeled and finely diced (2 cups)

120 ml dry white wine (e.g., Fendant* or Sauvignon Blanc)
(½ cup)

160 g leeks, finely chopped
(2 cups)

1 small handful fresh parsley, finely chopped (optional)

1 pinch nutmeg

½ teaspoon salt

freshly ground black pepper, to taste

80 ml light cream (⅓ cup)

80 ml milk (⅓ cup)

1 large egg

1 large egg white

200 g Raclette cheese, finely chopped (7 oz)

TOPPING:

1 large egg yolk

1 teaspoon milk

1 teaspoon poppyseeds

*In Valais, wine made with the Chasselas variety of grapes is called Fendant.

INSTRUCTIONS:

1. **Prepare the pastry dough.** Add the flour and salt to a large bowl. Add the cold butter in pieces. Use a pastry blender or two knives to cut the butter pieces into the flour until they become the size of small pebbles. Make a well in the center and add the cold water. Stir everything together to form a dough. Shape the dough into a disk, wrap it in parchment paper and refrigerate for 30–60 minutes. While the dough chills, prepare the filling.

2. **Prepare the filling.** Add the chopped bacon to a large frying pan over medium-high heat. Brown the meat, stirring frequently. Then take the pan off the heat. Tilt it to the side and carefully spoon out the grease.

3. Return the frying pan with the bacon to the stove over medium heat and add the potatoes and wine. Cook for about 5 minutes. Then add the leeks to the pan and cook for another 5 minutes, stirring occasionally, until they have softened. Add the chopped parsley and nutmeg. Stir everything together until well combined and season with salt and pepper. Add the filling to a large bowl and let it cool.

4. While the filling cools, take the pastry dough out of the refrigerator. On a new piece of parchment paper, roll out about two-thirds of the dough into a circle to fit the bottom and sides of a 28 cm (11 in) round tart pan with 1–2 cm extra dough around the outside (to be folded over the pastry lid). Then lift the dough on the parchment paper into the pan and press it into the bottom and sides. Let the excess dough fall over the outside of the pan. Prick the bottom of the dough with a fork. Place the pan and the remaining dough back in the refrigerator to cool for 5 minutes.

5. Add the cream, milk, egg, egg white and grated cheese to the large bowl with the leek and potato mixture. Stir everything together until well combined.

6. **Assemble the pie.** Take the pan and the remaining dough out of the refrigerator. Spread the filling evenly into the pan. Then roll out the remaining dough on the parchment paper to fit the top of the pie. Invert the parchment paper to place the dough lid on top of the filling. Then fold the excess pastry from the sides over the top of the pastry lid to seal in the filling. After that, cut a 2 ½ cm (1 in) circle in the lid to create a hole for the steam to escape.

7. **Prepare the topping.** Whisk together the egg yolk and milk until fully combined. Then use a pastry brush to spread a thin layer of this egg wash on the surface of the tart. Sprinkle evenly with poppyseeds.

8. Bake the pie for 35–45 minutes at 200°C (400°F) until its surface becomes golden brown. Let it cool slightly before serving.

Make-ahead tips:
Make the pastry dough in the morning and leave it in the refrigerator until you are ready to use it in the evening.

THE OTHER POTATO PIE FROM VALAIS (NOT CHOLERA!)

CANTON VALAIS

When you hear someone refer to the Gâteau Saviésan (a.k.a. Tarte Savièsanne or Gâteau Savièse) you might think they are talking about the sweet tart from the Savièse region of Valais. This French-speaking region includes over a dozen villages along the hillside above the cantonal capital of Sion. However, if it is that sweet tart that comes to mind, you would be wrong. Known as the *Flon de Savièse*, it is made with a short crust pastry filled with sliced fruit such as apples, apricots or plums and with a *sablé* (streusel) topping. The Gâteau Saviésan from the same region is actually a savory pie, traditionally made with a short crust or puff pastry filled with potatoes, leeks, cheese and bacon.

To confuse matters even more, this regional pie has a cousin in the German-speaking Valais with the unusual name of Choléra. Another savory pie, it has a filling almost identical to the Gâteau Saviésan, but the addition of sliced apples gives it a bit of sweetness. Some think the name comes from the bacterial disease that swept through Valais in the early 19th century. During that time, people stayed at home and cooked with simple ingredients that were

available. Others suggest the name comes from the regional term for coal (Chole), linked to how the pie was baked in a pot placed in the coals of a fire.

In a 1929 recipe booklet, Basile Luyet writes about *"l'art culinaire à Savièse"* (the art of cooking in Savièse). Though he does not specifically name the Gâteau Saviésan in the section about *gâteaux* (cakes), he describes cakes that pair potatoes with other ingredients, such as cheese, leeks and bacon. These early cakes certainly sound like the precursor to what we know today as the Gâteau Saviésan.

CHURER FLEISCHTORTE

CHUR MEAT PIE

One of my favorite recipes in this cookbook, this meat pie gets its name from Chur, the capital city of Graubünden. To assemble this pie, use the same method as the Gâteau Saviésan (p. 183). I enjoy eating it hot or cold with lots of hot sauce. It is another recipe that helps you use up stale bread.

Servings: 6–8

Prep: about 1 ¼ hours
(incl. time for the dough to chill)
Bake: 40–45 mins

INGREDIENTS:

PASTRY DOUGH:

220 g all-purpose flour (1 ¾ cups)

125 g spelt flour (1 ¼ cups)

1 teaspoon salt

125 g unsalted butter, cold
(½ cup)

2 tablespoons canola, rapeseed
or vegetable oil

120–150 ml water, cold
(½ to ⅔ cup)

FILLING:

75 g stale bread (1–2 slices)

150 ml milk (⅔ cup)

450–500 g ground beef
(about 1 lb)

1 large onion, finely chopped
(1 cup)

1 clove garlic, minced

1 teaspoon salt

½ teaspoon dried thyme

½ teaspoon dried marjoram

freshly ground black pepper, to
taste

150 g frozen spinach (5 oz)

60 ml red wine (¼ cup)

1 large egg white

1 tablespoon light cream (optional)

EGG WASH:

1 large egg yolk

2 teaspoons milk

SERVING SUGGESTION:

your favorite hot sauce

INSTRUCTIONS:

1. Add the stale bread to the milk. Let it soak for 30 minutes or until fully softened. Use a fork to break up the bread into small pieces so that it becomes like a thick paste. Refrigerate until you are ready to use it.

2. **Prepare the pastry dough.** Add the flours and salt to a large bowl. Add the cold butter in pieces. Use a pastry blender or two knives to cut the butter pieces into the flour until they are the size of small pebbles. Make a well in the center and add the oil and cold water. Stir everything together to form a dough. Shape the dough into a disk, wrap it in parchment paper and refrigerate for 30–60 minutes. While the dough chills, prepare the filling.

3. **Prepare the filling.** Add the ground beef to a large frying pan over medium-high heat. Brown the meat, stirring frequently and breaking it into small pieces. If needed, take the pan off the heat, tilt it to the side and carefully spoon out the liquid into a small bowl. Let it cool before discarding.

4. Return the frying pan to the stove over medium heat. Add the onion and cook for about 5 minutes or until it becomes translucent. Then stir in the garlic, salt, thyme, marjoram and black pepper and cook for another minute. Add the frozen spinach and cook for 5–10 minutes until it has completely thawed and is evenly distributed. Then stir in the milk and bread mixture. Next, add the red wine and stir until everything is fully combined.

5. Take the pan off the heat and add the meat filling to a heat–proof bowl to cool. While the filling cools, assemble the pie.

6. **Assemble the pie.** Take the pastry dough out of the refrigerator. On a new piece of parchment paper, roll out about two-thirds of the dough in a circle to fit the bottom and sides of a 28 cm (11 in) round tart pan, with about 1–2 cm of extra dough all around the outside (to be folded over the pastry lid). Then lift the dough on the parchment paper into the pan and press it into the bottom and sides. Let the excess dough fall over the outside of the pan. Prick the bottom of the dough with a fork.

7. Stir the egg white into the cooled meat filling in the large bowl and add the light cream, if the mixture seems a bit dry. Then, add the filling to the pan. Roll out the remaining dough on a piece of parchment paper to fit the top of the pie. Invert the parchment paper to place the dough lid on top of the filling. Then fold the excess pastry from the sides over the top of the pastry lid to seal it.

8. Whisk together the egg yolk and milk until well combined. Then use a pastry brush to spread a thin layer of this egg wash on the top of the pie. After that, use a fork to prick the pastry lid in several places. Bake the pie for 35–45 minutes at 200°C (400°F) until the surface becomes golden brown. Serve warm or cold.

Make-ahead tips:
Mix the bread with the milk in the morning and refrigerate until you are ready to use it.

Make the pastry dough in the morning and leave it in the refrigerator until you are ready to assemble the pie in the evening.

Cook the filling in the morning, cool to room temperature and refrigerate until you are ready to assemble the pie.

A TASTY MEAT PIE FROM SWITZERLAND'S OLDEST CITY

CANTON
GRAUBÜNDEN

With a history stretching back over 5,000 years, Chur has earned the title of Switzerland's oldest city. It is also the cantonal capital of Graubünden. To some, Chur may be viewed as a place you pass through on the way to more well-known tourist destinations in the canton, such as St. Moritz. However, I think Chur absolutely warrants a visit, particularly for its culinary specialties that you will not find anywhere else in Switzerland. These include Churer Röteli, a vibrant cherry liqueur, and Pfirsichsteine, marzipan-like candies shaped like peach stones.

When I visited Chur's historic city center in 2021, I wandered through the Saturday market stalls lining the narrow streets. This was only my second or third time in the city, and I remembered a special bakery I had previously visited that is known as the birthplace of Pfirsichsteine. On a mission to buy their famous candy, I returned to Bühler's Zuckerbäckerei. It is situated near the Obertor, one of three remaining towers from Chur's medieval walled fortifications. Master confectioner Otto Hürsch-Müller created the Pfirsichsteine here in 1887. This establishment is the city's oldest bakery.

Soon after I entered the bakery, I gleefully spotted another Churer specialty I had been wanting to try for years—the Fleischtorte (meat cake)! The triangular slice I bought had a pastry heart baked into its surface.

The Churer Fleischtorte is primarily made by professional bakers but is also made by home cooks. Recipes for the filling typically include a stale *Weggli*, a white bread roll I know in French-speaking Switzerland as a *Petit pain au lait* (little milk bread). I have added spinach to the filling in my recipe to replace some of the meat with a green vegetable. There are a million ways to make this delicious pie, so please adapt this recipe to make it your own.

SPECKKUCHEN

BACON FLATBREAD

The Speckkuchen is like a flatbread, traditionally topped with cream, bacon cubes and caraway seeds. My twist on the traditional recipe includes thinly sliced zucchini. I also use some whole wheat flour in the dough. Serve it for an apéro or for supper. To make a vegetarian version, just omit the bacon.

Servings: 4 (makes 3 cakes)

Prep: 2 ½ hours (incl. time for the dough to rise)
Bake: 15–20 mins per cake

INGREDIENTS:

DOUGH:

20 g fresh yeast, crumbled, or 8 g active dry yeast (2 ¼ teaspoons)

325 ml water, lukewarm (1 ⅓ cups)

250 g all-purpose or bread flour (2 cups)

250 g whole wheat flour (2 ¼ cups)

2 teaspoons salt

FILLING:

250 ml crème fraiche (1 cup) or 120 ml heavy cream, whipped (½ cup)

2–3 zucchini, very thinly sliced

75 g bacon, chopped (optional) (about 6 slices)

2–3 tablespoons caraway seeds

salt, to taste

Make-ahead tips:
Make the dough in the morning, let it sit on the counter for 20–30 minutes and then refrigerate all day in a covered bowl. Take it out of the refrigerator about 1 hour before you plan to use it so it can warm up. After that, continue from step 4 of the recipe.

INSTRUCTIONS:

1. In a small bowl, add the yeast to the lukewarm water. Let it sit for a few minutes and then stir until the yeast has completely dissolved.

2. Whisk the flours and salt together in a large bowl. Make a well in the center and add the yeast mixture. Stir the ingredients together to form a dough. Knead the dough for about 10 minutes by hand on a lightly floured surface, or using an electric mixer with a dough hook, until the dough becomes smooth and elastic.

3. Place the dough in the same large bowl and cover it with a damp kitchen towel. Let the dough rise at room temperature for 1–2 hours until it has doubled in size.

4. When the dough has risen, divide it into 3 equal balls. On a piece of parchment paper, roll out each ball into a circle with a diameter of about 30 cm (12 in) and a thickness of about 3 mm (1/10 in). Then, place each circle on a baking sheet. Prick the surface of the dough with a fork. Then spread the cream evenly on top and add a layer of the sliced zucchini, followed by the bacon, and then the caraway seeds and salt. Bake at 200°C (400°F) for 15–20 minutes, until the bacon is cooked and the edges of the crust are golden brown. Cut into triangles and serve.

A BACON FLATBREAD BORN IN COMMUNAL OVENS

CANTON FRIBOURG

Switzerland, and particularly French-speaking Switzerland, has a tradition of thin yeasted cakes or flatbreads that grew out of baking in communal wood-fired ovens. These cakes, made of rolled out pieces of bread dough, were used to test the temperature of the oven to see if it was ready for baking leavened loaves. Eventually, people started putting toppings on the flat dough to create sweet and savory cakes.

Several bilingual or German-speaking communities in the Seeland region of Fribourg, straddling the Röstigraben (p. 83), have two of Switzerland's thinnest versions of these cakes. One is the Salzkuchen (salt cake), a thin round bread dough first spread with whipped heavy cream and then sprinkled with salt, bacon and caraway seeds before it goes in the oven. True to its name, this cake is quite salty! At the bakeries in Kerzers, they make this cake with a special fatty white bacon.

In addition to the bakeries that make Salzkuchen, some villages in these communities still have a functioning communal oven, housed in buildings known as *Ofenhäuser* (oven houses), where they make these cakes. The wood-fired ovens are available from time to time for community events. For example, the Ofenhaus Münchenwiler has hosted a special Salzkuchenessen (salt cake meal) for decades. Next door to Kerzers in the village of Fräschels, the local chapter of the Fribourg Farmers' and Rural Women's Association organizes baking days throughout the year, such as the Salzkuchentage (salt cake days).

A similar cake found in this same region is called Speckkuchen (bacon cake). At the Krähenbühl bakery in Kerzers, they make their Speckkuchen with bacon cubes, caraway seeds and cheese. The main difference between the two cakes is that the Speckkuchen contains cubed bacon, while the Salzkuchen only has white bacon. This is why I use the term Speckkuchen for my recipe, to which I have added thinly sliced zucchini. A slice of this cake tastes best straight from the oven!

41 SMEAZZA

SAVORY SPINACH & LEEK CAKE

Other than chopping the vegetables, there is not a lot to do for this crustless vegetable cake, so it can be thrown together quickly for a weeknight supper. Serve it with sliced tomatoes and some crusty bread. It also works very well as a side dish for ham or sausages.

Servings: 4–6

Prep: 20–30 mins
Bake: 30–40 mins

INGREDIENTS:

1 tablespoon unsalted butter

1 medium onion, finely chopped (½ cup)

150 g leeks (white and green parts), finely chopped (2 cups)

250 g fresh spinach, finely chopped (½ lb)

1 small handful fresh parsley, finely chopped

1 small handful fresh basil, finely chopped (or 1 teaspoon dried basil)

120 ml milk (½ cup)

100 g Gruyère (or other cheese), cut into small cubes (generous ¾ cup)

60 g buckwheat flour (½ cup)

40 g all-purpose flour (⅓ cup)

1 large egg

½ teaspoon salt

¼ teaspoon black pepper

¼ teaspoon nutmeg

1 tablespoon olive oil

INSTRUCTIONS:

1. Line a 23 cm (9 in) round pan (ideally a springform pan) with parchment paper.

2. Melt the butter in a frying pan over medium heat. Add the onions and leeks and cook them for about 5 minutes, stirring occasionally, until the onions become translucent. Then, add them to a large bowl with the remaining ingredients except the olive oil. Mix everything together until evenly distributed.

3. Put the filling into the prepared pan, making sure the surface is flat and relatively even. Drizzle the tablespoon of olive oil over the top. Bake for 30–40 minutes at 200°C (400°F) until the cake has set and the surface has very lightly browned.

VEGETABLE CAKE FROM THE ITALIAN-SPEAKING MESOLCINA VALLEY

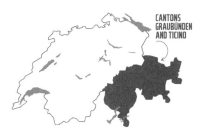

CANTONS GRAUBÜNDEN AND TICINO

Valle Mesolcina is one of four Italian-speaking valleys in Graubünden, Switzerland's largest canton by area. The valley borders Ticino to the west and Italy to the east. Running through the valley is the Moesa river, which starts in the San Bernadino mountain pass and flows down into the Ticino River. You will find a rustic, savory spinach cake called Smeazza in both Graubünden and Ticino.

Held together with buckwheat flour, eggs and cheese, Smeazza somewhat resembles a crustless vegetable quiche. The cookbook, *Ticino A Tavola* (Ticino at the Table, 1998), describes Smeazza as a *torta di verdure* (vegetable cake) from the Mesolcina Valley. Authors Maryton Guidicelli and Luigi Bosia include borage in their recipe. Both cultivated and grown in the wild, this edible plant's hairy leaves are used for cooking. Its blue flowers are added to salads and used as a colorful garnish. An article in *Terra Grischuna* magazine (Graubünden Soil, 2017) about traditional culinary specialties from this region also defines Smeazza as "a

flat vegetable cake with buckwheat flour and borage." It explains that the wild herbs and vegetables helped to make the local dishes healthier and less monotonous.

A similar dish from Ticino goes by the name Scarpazza. Made with Swiss chard, spinach and stale bread, it also includes eggs and cheese as a binder. It more closely resembles a gratin than Smeazza, but the dishes can be quite similar. You may also see Scarpazza referred to as Torta di Frà (Friar's Cake).

In the *Almanacco del Grigioni Italiano* (2010), the Italian language almanac for Graubünden, there is a first-person account from Reto Binda of living in the Mesolcina Valley during World War II. He writes about his aunt Margheritin serving roasted chestnuts or bread with homemade Smeazza. These old dishes made by mothers, grandmothers and aunts, lovingly prepared with simple ingredients, evoke memories of generations before us.

BÄRNER CHÄSCHÜECHLI

BERN CHEESE TARTLETS

I love little Swiss cheese tarts. You can find them throughout the country, with different names and made with a variety of cheeses. My recipe connects this dish to the canton of Bern, the birthplace of Switzerland's famous Emmentaler cheese.

Servings: 4–8 (makes 8 tartlets)

Prep: about 1 hour
(incl. time for the dough to rest)
Bake: 20–30 mins

INGREDIENTS:

DOUGH:

125 g all-purpose flour (1 cup)

75 g whole wheat flour (⅔ cup)

¼ teaspoon salt

75 g unsalted butter, cold
(⅓ cup)

4–5 tablespoons water, cold

FILLING:

175 g Emmentaler, grated
(1 ½ cups)

100 g Gruyère, grated
(scant 1 cup)

3 large eggs

60 ml milk (¼ cup)

60 ml plain yogurt (¼ cup)

¼ teaspoon salt

1 handful fresh herbs, such as
thyme, sage or parsley

INSTRUCTIONS:

1. **Prepare the pastry dough.** Whisk the two flours together with the salt in a large bowl. Add the cold butter in pieces. Use a pastry blender or two knives to cut the butter pieces into the flour mixture until they become the size of small pebbles. Make a well in the center and add the cold water. Stir everything together to form a dough. Shape the dough into a disk, wrap it in parchment paper and refrigerate for 30–60 minutes.

2. When the dough has chilled, grease 8 tartlet pans with a diameter of 9–10 cm (3 ½–4 in). Take the dough out of the refrigerator and divide it into 8 pieces. Form one into a ball and roll it out on a lightly floured surface until about 3–4 mm (about ¼ in) thick. Press the dough into the bottom and sides of one of the pans. Roll the rolling pin over the top of the pan to cut off any excess dough. Prick the bottom of the dough with a fork. Repeat this process with the remaining pieces of dough, then place the pans in the refrigerator to chill.

3. **Prepare the filling.** Add all the ingredients to a large bowl, except for the fresh herbs. Stir everything together until well combined. Take the pans out of the refrigerator and carefully spoon the filling into them. Gently lay some sprigs and leaves of the fresh herbs on top.

4. Bake the tartlets on the bottom rack of the oven for 20–25 minutes at 200°C (400°F). The pastry should be lightly browned, and the filling should be fully set and golden.

Variations:
Feel free to change the types of cheese you use with this recipe, but I recommend sticking to hard or semi-hard cheeses.

You can add small quantities of finely chopped vegetables, such as leftover steamed broccoli or fresh spinach, to the pans before you spoon in the egg and cheese mixture. You may need to bake the tarts longer, depending on how much you add.

Make-ahead tips:
Make the dough in the morning and leave it in the refrigerator until you are ready to use it in the evening.

You can also grate the cheese in advance and refrigerate it until you are ready to make the filling.

MY FAVORITE LITTLE SWISS CHEESE TARTS

CANTON BERN

Chäschüechli (cheese tartlets) resemble mini quiches but with a lot more cheese! When I travel in Switzerland and need a quick lunch from a bakery, I will often buy one. They have a higher ratio of pastry to filling in comparison to their larger versions. Bakers make them with either puff pastry or short crust pastry. In French-speaking Switzerland, they are often called *ramequins*.

The first time I made my own Chäschüechli was during a Swiss cheese course at Sherly's Kitchen in Zurich's Wollishofen neighborhood. Since moving to Switzerland after having previously lived in Seoul, Manila and San Francisco, Sherly has become a certified cheese sommelier, passing the rigorous Käse-Sommelier course at Die Weinausbildung in Nuolen in the canton of Schwyz. I remember thinking during the course how easy it was to make something I had always purchased at a bakery.

Over the years, I developed my own recipe for Chäschüechli. I add whole wheat flour to the dough for a bit more flavor and texture. Instead of cream, I only use milk. In terms of cheese, I generally add a mix of Emmentaler and Gruyère. Otherwise, I just use up whatever cheese I have left in my refrigerator!

Having originated in the canton of Bern, Emmentaler today is also made by cheesemakers in other Swiss cantons. Of course, this cheese is well known around the world for its holes. In 2015, Agroscope, the Swiss center of excellence for agricultural research, issued a press release provocatively titled, "Riddle of Hole Formation in Cheese Solved." Their research indicated a link between the presence of hay particles and the number of holes in this cheese.

In the same year that this important fact was uncovered, an article with another attention-grabbing title appeared on Blick.ch, an online tabloid: "Machen Chäschüechli dick?" (Do cheese tartlets make us fat?) In the article, nutritionist Claudia Müller describes them as a "calorie bomb." She adds that each tartlet consumed requires at least a 50-minute walk to burn them off. Perhaps this is why the Swiss routinely serve them with a fresh salad!

KÄSESCHNITTEN / CROÛTES AU FROMAGE

CHEESE TOASTS WITH MUSHROOMS & WATERCRESS

Something like open–faced grilled cheese sandwiches, Käseschnitten are the perfect last-minute supper. I like topping them with sauteed mushrooms and watercress, but there are lots of other ways you can make them (e.g., with a slice of ham, topped with steamed broccoli or a fried egg).

Servings: 3–4

Prep: about 15 mins
Bake: 10–15 mins

INGREDIENTS:

CHEESE SLICES:

2 tablespoons unsalted butter

5–7 slices of stale bread

325 g cheese (Gruyère, Vacherin Fribourgeois, Emmentaler, etc.), grated (about 3 cups)

60 ml milk (¼ cup)

1 large egg

1 tablespoon all-purpose flour

freshly ground black pepper, to taste

MUSHROOM TOPPING:

1 tablespoon olive oil

300–350 g mixed mushrooms (chanterelles, button mushrooms, shiitake, etc.), sliced (4–4 ½ cups)

1 small handful fresh tarragon, chives or parsley, finely chopped

a large handful of fresh watercress

salt and pepper, to taste

INSTRUCTIONS:

1. Place the slices of bread on a baking sheet lined with parchment paper. Butter the top of the bread.

2. Add the cheeses, milk, egg, flour and pepper to a large bowl and stir until well-combined. Top the slices of bread evenly with the cheese mixture, pressing it down slightly to fix it in place. Then bake them in an oven heated to 200°C (400°F) for about 10 minutes until the cheese has fully melted and become lightly browned. While they bake, prepare the mushrooms.

3. Add the oil to a large skillet over medium heat and cook the mushrooms until just softened (5–10 minutes). Sprinkle with salt and pepper, to taste. Then add the tarragon, chives or parsley to the skillet and stir until well-combined. Keep the mixture warm until the cheese toasts are out of the oven.

4. When the cheese toasts are ready, top them with the sauteed mushrooms. Then add the fresh watercress on top and serve immediately.

SWITZERLAND'S OPEN-FACED MELTED CHEESE SANDWICH

THROUGHOUT SWITZERLAND

Käseschnitte (cheese slice) in German or Croûte au fromage (cheese crust) in French and Crostoni al formaggio (cheese toast) in Italian involves covering stale bread with a layer of melted cheese to create the ultimate comfort meal. Super-fast and super-convenient, there are a million variations. Even though this cheese dish is just as popular in Switzerland as fondue and raclette, I find it less well-known outside the country.

I often associate Käseschnitte with Alpine restaurants, sometimes only accessible by foot, where you arrive wearing your backpack and your hiking boots. The friendly server brings the steaming hot dish to your table, straight from the oven. The slice of bread is sometimes so coated in liquid cheese that it seems more like a thick soup. To make Käseschnitte, grated cheese is mixed with an egg and other ingredients, or sliced cheese is layered on the bread, maybe with a fried egg placed on top. It nearly always comes with cornichons and pickled onions—their sharp acidity helps cut through the richness of the cheese.

To revive your stale bread, you can drizzle white wine or beer over it before you put on the cheese topping, but this can make the bread very soft and wet when you bake it. Swiss French TV personality and author, Jacques Montandon, presented his *jurassienne* version of this dish in 1982 on his program, *Les petits plats sur l'écran* (small dishes on the screen). He removed the crusts from the bread and then fried them in a pan with a very generous amount of butter. Finally, he poured an abundant splash of white wine over the bread slices in a baking dish before adding the cheese mixture. No wonder the bread sometimes gets lost!

I prefer that the bread keep some of its texture, so I leave the crusts on, try to use less butter, and omit the wine altogether— although I add some milk. If your bread is super dry and you are opening a bottle of white wine or a beer for supper, it certainly would not hurt to sprinkle some on, but I will leave that decision up to you! And feel free to experiment with whatever cheese or other toppings you have in your refrigerator, like leftover sliced ham, steamed broccoli or chopped spinach.

WURSTWEGGEN

SAUSAGE ROLLS

For people not familiar with Wurstweggen, you could describe them as meat-filled pastry batons. The filling can vary widely, depending on who makes them. This recipe with pork and apple has become a family favorite. Make the pastry yourself (recipe at cuisinehelvetica.com) or use store-bought puff pastry.

Servings: 4–8 (8 sausage rolls)

Prep: about 30 mins (not including the pastry)
Bake: 15–20 mins

INGREDIENTS:

FILLING:

3 teaspoons fennel seeds

1 tablespoon unsalted butter

1 medium onion, finely chopped (½ cup)

1 clove garlic, minced

300 g ground pork (⅔ lb)

½ teaspoon dried sage

¾ teaspoon salt

1 small apple, grated (½ cup)

2 tablespoons breadcrumbs (p. 17)

freshly ground black pepper, to taste

1 small handful fresh parsley, finely chopped

PASTRY:

Homemade puff pastry or about 320 g store–bought puff pastry

INSTRUCTIONS:

1. In a medium frying pan over medium heat, toast the fennel seeds for a few minutes until fragrant, stirring frequently, then add the butter. When the butter has melted, add the onion and garlic. Cook for about 5 minutes, stirring occasionally, until the onion becomes translucent. Take the pan off the heat and let the mixture cool slightly.

2. Transfer the onion mixture to a large bowl, add the remaining filling ingredients and stir everything together until well combined.

3. If you make your own dough: Roll out the puff pastry dough to make one large rectangle about 28 x 38 cm (11 x 15 in). Cut the dough into 8 rectangles. Then roll out each rectangle again so they measure about 14 x 18 cm (5 ½ x 7 in).

    If you use store-bought dough: Cut the rectangle of dough into 8 rectangles and then roll out each rectangle again to roughly match the dimensions listed above.

4. Take one of the rectangles and place 3–4 tablespoons of the meat filling in the center of the right side and spread it out to create a long, thin cylinder (see illustration on p. 208). Make sure to leave about a 2 cm (¾ in) gap between the filling and the edges of the dough. Brush a thin layer of the beaten egg on these edges with a pastry brush. Carefully fold the left side of the dough over the right side so

the sides match up evenly. Press the edges
of the dough with the tines of a fork to seal
them. Then gently lift the pastry onto a baking
sheet lined with parchment paper. Repeat this
process with the remaining rectangles.

5. Brush the surface of the Wurstweggen with
    the beaten egg. Bake for 18–25 minutes at
    200°C (400°F) until the pastry has turned
    golden brown and the filling is fully cooked.

Make-ahead tip:
Prepare the pastry and/or filling in the morning
or afternoon and refrigerate until you are
ready to use it in the evening.

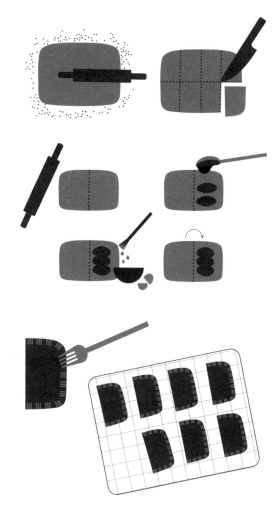

SWITZERLAND'S MEAT-FILLED PASTRY BATONS

SUISSE ALÉMANIQUE

One evening in Fribourg, I mentioned to the people sitting around me that I had just made Wurstweggen. None of them seemed to have heard of this dish before. It was likely because of my accent. They thought I was referring to something vegan, as this Swiss German word is pronounced "vorst-vegg-en."

Not vegan at all, Wurstweggen resemble English sausage rolls in that they do not contain an actual sausage—except for the Schüblingweggen in Schaffhausen. Instead, they have a ground meat filling surrounded by puff pastry. The narrow rectangular pastry has its filling slightly exposed at each end (although I completely enclose it when I make them). From my experience, they are more commonly made today by professional bakers than in home kitchens. You will find them with other hot food for take-out at bakeries, supermarkets and gas stations.

Even though you can generally find them throughout the country, although less so in the Italian-speaking regions, they are most common in German-speaking Switzerland.

In French-speaking regions, meat filled pastries typically take the form of *rissoles* or *chaussons*, shaped like half-moons, or *pâté à la viande*, muffin-shaped pastries with a small circle of meat jelly exposed on top.

The canton of Aargau seems to particularly like the Wurstweggen, since it figures in two annual celebrations. The first is the Zofinger Kinderfest, held in the town of Zofingen on the first Friday in July. Schoolchildren receive a special Kinderfestweggen for lunch, made with ingredients such as beef, veal, onions and breadcrumbs. The second is in Lenzburg during the Chlausmarkt (Christmas market). A meeting of the mayors and other officials from the nearly two dozen municipalities always includes Wurstweggen as part of the refreshments.

You can fill the puff pastry with whatever ingredients you prefer—meat or vegetables—they will be popular with kids and politicians alike!

SWEET SUPPERS

Switzerland has a history of making sweet dishes for supper, predominantly in its German-speaking regions. It might seem somewhat odd, but this practice is not entirely unfamiliar to me. Growing up in the US, from time to time my family's evening meal would be "breakfast for supper." When my children were young, I did the same thing—often a last-minute decision when I ran out of ideas or the time to cook. Typically, this meant I would make fluffy American pancakes.

Sweet suppers certainly are not just for kids! Serving breakfast-inspired dishes like this breaks up the normal routine of suppertime. It may seem silly, but a sweet switch-up can add a bit of fun to the meal. And sometimes you just have to celebrate the small things in life with something sweet—perhaps by baking a pear tart from Geneva (p. 241) for a weeknight supper.

Every recipe in this chapter incorporates some type of fruit, either in the dish or served on the side. Apples appear most often, but you will also find pears, plums and quince. Where possible, I have reduced the added sugar to allow the fruit to provide the sweetness. This chapter also features several types of grains and cereals, such as whole wheat flour, rolled oats and semolina. Two of the recipes will help you use up stale bread—Apfelrösti, a skillet bread and apple dish (p. 213), and Fotzelschnitten (p. 221), the Swiss German recipe for what I know as French toast.

Even though these recipes work well as an evening meal, you can also serve them for breakfast or lunch, or as a snack or dessert. If you have a sweet tooth like me, these recipes are especially for you!

45 APFELRÖSTI

FRIED APPLES & BREAD

Thinly sliced stale bread toasted in a pan with sliced apples and raisins or dried cranberries takes only minutes to throw together. Serve this dish with some hard-boiled eggs and a green salad and you have a superfast sweet and savory supper.

Servings: 4

Prep: 10–15 mins
Cook: about 15 mins

INGREDIENTS:

5–7 slices stale bread

1 tablespoon lemon juice

1 tablespoon orange juice

2 large apples (e.g., Gala, Cox's Orange or Braeburn)

2–3 tablespoons dried cranberries, raisins or dried currants

1 tablespoon sugar

zest ½ organic orange

1 dash cinnamon

2–3 tablespoons unsalted butter

TO GARNISH:

1 handful whole almonds (or walnuts), roughly chopped

INSTRUCTIONS:

1. Cut the bread into thin slices and then into bite-sized pieces. Set aside.

2. Add the lemon and orange juice to a large bowl. Thinly slice the apples, place them in the bowl immediately and toss with the citrus juices to prevent the slices from turning brown. Then stir in the dried cranberries, sugar, orange zest and cinnamon.

3. Melt the butter in a large frying pan over medium-high heat. Add the bread pieces to the pan, coating them on all sides with the butter. Fry them for about 5 minutes or until golden brown. Then add the apples and juice to the pan, stirring until they become well distributed. Put a lid on the pan and simmer for another 5–10 minutes, stirring occasionally. When the apples have softened, sprinkle with the chopped almonds and serve immediately.

RÖSTI MADE WITH APPLES AND BREAD

SUISSE ALÉMANIQUED

"Altes Brot ist nicht hart — kein Brot, das ist hart!"
(Old bread is not hard — no bread, that is hard!)
– Proverb

Switzerland has over 200 different types of bread. So, it should come as no surprise that there are a lot of Swiss recipes that use up old bread. Even so, significant quantities of bread unfortunately end up as household waste every year. A study carried out by the Federal Institute of Technology Zurich estimates that 40 kilograms of bread and baked goods per person are thrown away each year in Switzerland.

To help address this issue, part of my goal with this book is to highlight both savory and sweet recipes that incorporate stale bread and breadcrumbs. Apfelrösti, also known as *Apfelbröisi*, falls under the sweet category of these dishes. Bite-sized pieces of bread are toasted in a frying pan with butter and apple slices. Raisins are often added to the mix, although I prefer this dish with dried cranberries or dried currants.

You can also add a dash of cinnamon or nutmeg or whatever spices you like. Leftover brioche-style loaves work well for this dish, or you can make it with a crusty white bread, such as Glarnerbrot (p. 222). When you add a batter made of eggs and milk to the pan, then the dish is called *Vogelheu* (bird's hay).

Apfelrösti is most often served at home, but you can also find it in Swiss restaurants from time to time. I remember seeing it on the menu at the restaurant of the historic Jugendstil-Hotel Paxmontana in the canton of Obwalden. Offered alongside their wild game menu for the fall, Apfelrösti was a nice seasonal addition to the dessert menu.

You too can easily make Apfelrösti at home and have fun adapting it to your taste. And it will help fight food waste at the same time!

BIRCHERMÜESLI

THE ORIGINAL "OVERNIGHT OATS"

In keeping with the original version of Birchermüesli developed in the early 20th century, my recipe features raw apple as the main ingredient. It works particularly well for supper on a hot summer's night when you may not feel like cooking.

Servings: 1

Prep: about 8 hours of refrigeration
Assemble: 5–10 mins

INGREDIENTS:

1 tablespoon rolled oats

2 tablespoons milk

1 apple (e.g., Gala, Braeburn or McIntosh)

1–2 tablespoons plain yogurt

1 teaspoon lemon juice, freshly squeezed (optional)

1–2 teaspoons flax seeds

TO GARNISH:

3 tablespoons walnuts, almonds or hazelnuts, chopped

1 small handful berries, fresh (if in season) or frozen (and thawed)

INSTRUCTIONS:

1. In the morning (or in the evening, if you are making it for breakfast), add the oats and milk to a cereal bowl. Cover and place in the refrigerator for about 8 hours.

2. Take the bowl out of the fridge. Grate the apple and stir it in along with the plain yogurt, lemon juice and flax seeds until well combined. Top with the chopped nuts and berries.

SWITZERLAND'S MOST FAMOUS CULINARY EXPORT?

CANTON ZURICH

Invented by Dr. Maximilian Oskar Bircher-Benner (1867–1939) at the turn of the 20th century, the original recipe for Birchermüesli features grated apple as its primary ingredient. *Müesli* means "little mush" in Swiss German—an effective way to describe the dish. Dr. Bircher-Benner, convinced that raw apples cured him of jaundice, developed this dish to combat what he viewed as poor nutritional habits brought on in part by the industrial revolution. He was reportedly inspired by something served to him while hiking in the mountains.

Dr. Bircher-Benner's original recipe for his Apfeldiätspeise (apple diet dish) paired oats soaked in water with grated apple, lemon juice, sweetened condensed milk and nuts. When mixed, he apparently believed these vital ingredients, which he also called "d'Spys" ("the food" in Swiss German), contained nutrients like those found in breast milk. His original recipe avoided fresh milk or cream for fear of contracting bovine tuberculosis.

In 1904, Dr. Bircher-Benner opened a sanitorium called Lebendige Kraft (Vital Force) on the hillside of the Zürichberg. Overlooking Lake Zurich, guests of this health facility willingly engaged in a holistic regime of early morning walks, vegetarian dining, sunlight therapy and early bedtimes. Birchermüesli was part of the package, for a snack or as a starter to the evening meal. I wonder if he ever imagined that his culinary invention would become known across the globe. Nowadays, Müesli can be found in most supermarkets as a dry cereal.

His niece, Dr. Dagmar Liechti-von Brasch, took over the sanitorium after his death, carrying on the teachings of her uncle. It was renamed Klinik Bircher-Benner in his memory and eventually closed in 1995. In Zurich, you can still find traces of Dr. Bircher-Benner. One summer's day, I got off the tram at the Kirche Fluntern stop and walked uphill in search of the former clinic. I knew I was heading in the right direction when I reached Bircher-Benner-Platz. Not long after, I arrived at the site, now owned by an insurance company. In the quiet garden just below the main building is a plaque in his honor.

GLARNERBROT FOTZELSCHNITTEN

SPICED FRENCH TOAST

Inspired by the canton of Glarus, my version of this French toast recipe calls for day-old slices of Glarnerbrot (p. 222) and powdered sandalwood, an ingredient in a Glarner spiced sugar known as Magenträs. Feel free to substitute with your favorite French toast bread.

Servings: 4

Prep: about 15 mins
Cook: 15–20 mins

INGREDIENTS:

180 ml milk (¾ cup)

3 large eggs

1 tablespoon sugar

1 teaspoon powdered sandalwood*

½ teaspoon vanilla paste or extract

¼ teaspoon cinnamon

¼ teaspoon nutmeg

¼ teaspoon ground cloves

¼ teaspoon ground ginger

1–2 tablespoons unsalted butter

8–10 slices day–old bread (e.g., Glarnerbrot, p. 222)

*If you cannot find sandalwood powder, you can omit this ingredient and increase the amount of cinnamon to 1 teaspoon. In lieu of all the spices, you can also substitute 1 tablespoon of Magenträs.

SERVING SUGGESTION:

applesauce or another fruit compote, such as quince puree (p. 238), or maple syrup.

INSTRUCTIONS:

1. Add the milk, eggs, sugar and spices to a large bowl. Whisk everything together until well combined to create a smooth, thin batter.

2. Melt the butter in a medium skillet over medium-high heat. Soak the bread in the egg mixture, turning the slices to make sure both sides are covered.

3. Fry the bread slices for several minutes on both sides until golden brown. Serve immediately.

GLARNERBROT
CANTONAL BREAD FOR GLARUS

You can use the crusty cantonal bread of Glarus to make several recipes in this book, such as Herbed Croutons (p. 21), Fotzelschnitten (p. 221) or Käseschnitten (p. 203), as well as turning leftover slices into breadcrumbs (p. 17) for recipes like Steak Vigneron (p. 165) and Schnetz ond Häppere (p. 85).

Servings: 6–8

Prep: about 2 ½ hours
Bake: 25–30 mins

INGREDIENTS:

20 g fresh yeast, crumbled, or 8 g active dry yeast (2 ¼ teaspoons)

300 water, lukewarm (1 ¼ cups)

500 g bread flour (4 cups)

9 g salt (1 ½ teaspoons)

INSTRUCTIONS:

1. In a small bowl, add the yeast and the lukewarm water. Let it sit for a few minutes and then stir until the yeast has dissolved.

2. In a large bowl, whisk together the flour and salt and make a well in the center. Pour the yeast mixture into the well and stir until a dough forms.

3. Knead the dough for about 10 minutes by hand on a lightly floured surface, or using an electric mixer with a dough hook, until the dough becomes smooth and elastic.

4. Place the dough in the same large bowl and cover it with a damp kitchen towel. Let it rise at room temperature for 1–2 hours or until it has doubled in size.

5. After the dough has risen, form it into an elongated oval shape about 25 cm (10 in) in length. Place it on a baking sheet lined with parchment paper. Dust the surface of the dough lightly with flour and cover it loosely with a clean kitchen towel. Let it rest at room temperature for 30 minutes.

6. After the dough has rested, remove the towel and place an oven-safe ramekin filled with some hot water in the corner of the baking sheet with the bread (to generate steam and produce a crustier loaf). Make a long slash, about 1 cm (½ in) deep, lengthwise in the bread. Then bake at 220°C (425°F) for 25–30 minutes until the surface has browned and it sounds hollow when tapped on the bottom. Cool on a wire rack.

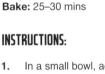

SANDALWOOD POWDER WITH THE CANTONAL BREAD FROM GLARUS

CANTON GLARUS

Magenträs, a spiced sugar from the canton of Glarus, stands out because of its unexpected coral hue. This regional specialty created in 1900 owes its color to a unique ingredient—powdered sandalwood. A popular way to enjoy Magenträs is to sprinkle some on a slice of buttered bread.

This inspired me to create a new recipe for French toast—known as *Fotzelschnitten* in German (*Schnitten* means "slices," but the old term *Fotzel* has several meanings) or *pain perdu* (lost bread) in French. It combines powdered sandalwood with Glarnerbrot (p. 222), the cantonal bread of Glarus. Another inspiration for my recipe is a similar dish made in Zurich with Magenträs known as Triätschnitten. Unlike a classic French toast, the bread slices in this dish are soaked in red wine. It is therefore more suited to dessert than to supper.

According to the *Schweizerisches Idiotikon*, a lexicon of the Swiss German language, the first documented evidence of spiced sugars in Switzerland comes from the 16th century. *Magen* means "stomach" and *Träs* is derived from *Trisenet*, which means something like "coarse powder." It received the name because it was once thought to aid digestion.

Glarnerbrot is a cantonal bread, one of 21 different types. Launched in 1950 at a trade fair in Lugano, these breads came about in part from a desire to preserve regional bread traditions. Examples of other cantonal breads include the wholesome rye bread from Valais (*Walliser Roggenbrot* in German or *Pain de seigle* valaisan in French) and the fluffy white Pane Ticinese from Ticino.

Did you know that Glarus has the smallest cantonal capital in Switzerland? Also called Glarus, the town had a population of about 6,200 as of January 1, 2024. If you ever travel there, be sure to pick up some Magenträs and Glarnerbrot for yourself! In the meantime, you can get a flavor for this canton at home when you make this easy sweet supper.

48 GRIESS-SCHNITTEN

SEMOLINA SLICES WITH STEWED PLUMS

You can tackle several steps of this recipe in advance to save time in the evening, such as cooking the semolina and spreading it out to cool. The stewed plums can also be made in advance. As an alternative to the plums, the semolina slices pair well with applesauce or maple syrup.

Servings: 6

INGREDIENTS:

750 ml milk (about 3 cups)

2 tablespoons sugar

1 teaspoon vanilla extract or paste

½ teaspoon salt

125 g coarse semolina (not semolina flour) (¾ cup)

1–2 tablespoons unsalted butter, melted

SERVING SUGGESTION:

stewed plums (p. 226), applesauce, quince puree (p. 238) or maple syrup

TO GARNISH:

pistachios, walnuts or almonds, etc., chopped

Prep: about 15 mins
+ 2 hours for the semolina to chill
Cook: 15–20 mins

INSTRUCTIONS:

1. Line a 22 x 30 cm (8 ½ x 12 in) rectangular baking sheet pan (ideally with a rolled edge and a lip around the pan) with parchment paper.

2. Add the milk to a medium saucepan and stir in the sugar, vanilla and salt. Bring to a boil over medium-high heat, stirring almost constantly, and then reduce the heat to medium. Slowly pour in the semolina, stirring constantly. Cook the semolina for 3–4 minutes, again stirring constantly, until it absorbs the milk and thickens. Then pour it into the prepared pan and spread the mixture out evenly; it should be about 1 cm (about ½ in) thick. Let it cool to room temperature. Cover and place in the refrigerator to cool for at least 2 hours.

3. Cut the sheet of cooled semolina into about 6 cm (2 ½ in) squares. Melt the butter in a large frying pan over medium-high heat. Cook the semolina squares on each side for 3–5 minutes until they turn golden brown. Serve immediately with the stewed plums (p. 226), or one of the other serving suggestions.

Make-ahead tip:
Complete steps 1 and 2 and then refrigerate the semolina for up to 2–3 days until you are ready to fry it on the stove in step 3.

STEWED PLUMS

A quick plum compote to serve with the Griess-Schnitten (p. 225) or Tatsch (p. 237).

Servings: 6

Prep: 5–10 mins
Cook: 25–35 mins

INGREDIENTS:

450–500 g fresh or frozen plums, halved and pitted (about 1 lb)

100 ml water (scant ½ cup)

3–4 tablespoons sugar

¼ teaspoon cinnamon

INSTRUCTIONS:

1. Add all the ingredients to a medium saucepan and bring to a boil. Lower the temperature to medium-low and simmer for 20–30 minutes until the plums are soft and fully cooked and the mixture has thickened slightly.

2. When the stewed plums are ready, serve them warm with the Griess-Schnitten. Alternatively, transfer them to a heat-safe container to cool to room temperature, then seal the container, refrigerate and serve them cold when the Griess-Schnitten are ready.

Make-ahead tip:
Prepare the stewed plums ahead of time and store in the refrigerator for up to 2–3 days.

SWEET SLICES OF SEMOLINA FOR SUPPER

SUISSE ALÉMANIQUE

Semolina routinely appears as an ingredient in the pasta we eat, but in Switzerland, you will also find it in sweet dishes. The term "semolina" describes the coarse middlings made from durum wheat (*Triticum durum*), which have a hard consistency. Before moving to Switzerland in 2012, I had never cooked with coarse semolina. My only experience was with fine semolina flour, which I had used to make homemade ravioli. Now, I routinely keep coarse semolina in my pantry.

In Switzerland, the majority of durum wheat is imported. As a result, the package of semolina from the supermarket might list one or several countries, such as Canada, the Czech Republic or Austria, for its place of origin. One of the largest producers of this crop is actually the Canadian province of Saskatchewan, where my maternal grandfather was born.

During the Covid-19 pandemic, it was reported that two major Swiss supermarkets were seeing higher than usual demand for semolina. This relatively inexpensive and shelf-stable ingredient works well for both sweet and savory recipes, so you can understand why people wanted to stock up on it during that time.

Like the pasta made from it, semolina can be a vehicle for a myriad of ingredients. When you see recipes for Griess-Schnitten (semolina slices), they could be for a dessert or a main dish. For example, the 2018 Swiss Army cookbook includes a basic recipe for savory semolina slices under the category "Stärkebeilagen" (starchy side dishes). The book offers several variations of this recipe by adding ingredients such as corn, seeds or tomatoes.

You can throw together a super quick supper if you cook the semolina in the morning and spread it out on a baking sheet to cool in the refrigerator during the day. Some recipes have you dip the semolina slices in beaten egg before frying, while others coat them in breadcrumbs. I have kept my recipe super simple to get you started. Please modify it to fit your preferences—the options are endless!

NIDWALDNER APFELAUFLAUF

NIDWALDEN APPLE SOUFFLE CASSEROLE

49

I usually describe this gently sweetened dish found in central Switzerland as an apple souffle casserole. To make it, you nestle sliced apples in a fluffy batter before baking. Feel free to spice up the batter with ingredients like cinnamon, vanilla or cardamom.

Servings: 6–8

Prep: about 30 mins
Bake: 30–35 mins

INGREDIENTS:

1 tablespoon lemon juice

2 tablespoons sugar

3–4 large baking apples (e.g., Granny Smith or Boskoop)

3 large eggs, separated

60 g all-purpose flour (½ cup)

150 ml milk (⅔ cup)

60 ml light cream (¼ cup)

1 pinch salt

TO GARNISH:

powdered sugar (optional)

INSTRUCTIONS:

1. Grease a 22 x 32 cm (8 ½ x 12 ½ in) rectangular ceramic baking dish.

2. Stir the lemon juice and 1 tablespoon of the sugar together in a medium bowl. Peel, halve and core the apples. Then immediately slice and toss them in the bowl with the lemon juice until well coated to prevent them from browning. Set aside.

3. Whisk together the remaining tablespoon of sugar with the egg yolks, flour, milk and cream in a medium bowl until these ingredients are evenly distributed and the mixture is smooth. Set aside.

4. In another large bowl, combine the egg whites with the salt. Using an electric mixer, beat until they become light, fluffy and form stiff peaks. Next, carefully fold them into the egg, milk and flour mixture until combined, but still fluffy.

5. Pour the batter into the prepared baking dish. After that, gently place the apple slices on top of the batter in an even layer. Bake at 180°C (350°F) for 30–35 minutes until the filling has set, the surface has lightly browned and the apples have softened. Serve while still warm, dusted with powdered sugar (optional).

A SUPER-EASY APPLE CASSEROLE

CANTON
NIDWALDEN

In German-speaking Switzerland, there is an entire category of dishes called *Auflauf*. This term refers to a baked dish, either sweet or savory. I consider the English equivalent of this dish to be something like a casserole.

Marianne Kaltenbach's 1977 seminal Swiss cookbook, *Ächti Schwizer Chuchi* (authentic Swiss cuisine) has a sweet Auflauf dish made with apples named *Apfelauflauf nach Grossmutterart* (Grandmother-style apple casserole). She described it as a Nidwaldner recipe, however recipes like this are not limited to this canton. While the Nidwalden version is almost like an apple souffle, other recipes for Apfelauflauf in Switzerland call for slices of stale bread and are almost like a baked French toast. One such recipe appears in another important Swiss cookbook, *Fülscher-Kochbuch* (1966) by author Elizabeth Fülscher. Her *Einfacher Apfelauflauf* (simple apple casserole) recipe incorporates bread in the form of Zwieback, a type of rusk.

To learn more about the Nidwaldner Apfelauflauf, I contacted the Culinarium Alpinum, Switzerland's competence center for Alpine cuisine. Located in a former Capuchin monastery in Stans, the capital of Nidwalden, this historic building also houses a restaurant and rooms for overnight guests. The restaurant sometimes has Nidwaldner Apfelauflauf on its menu, served as a dessert with vanilla sauce. Corine Niederberger, who grew up in Nidwalden and works at the Culinarium Alpinum, told me that dishes like the Apfelauflauf were prepared when people could only afford to cook with the ingredients they had on hand. The ingredients they used were mostly from their own farm or their neighbor's.

When you make this dish at home, the smell of baked apples will permeate your kitchen. Make sure to eat it soon after it comes out of the oven or the golden filling around the apples will start to deflate!

RHABARBERWÄHE

RHUBARB TART

This classic Swiss tart combines rhubarb with a vanilla-scented custard filling. The season for rhubarb always seems to pass by quickly, so bake this tart while you can!

Servings: 6–8

Prep: 20–30 mins
+ 30–60 mins for refrigeration
Bake: 35–45 mins

INGREDIENTS:

DOUGH:

125 g all-purpose flour (1 cup)

75 g whole wheat flour (⅔ cup)

¼ teaspoon salt

85 g unsalted butter, cold (6 tablespoons)

1 large egg, lightly beaten

2–3 tablespoons cold water

FILLING:

30 g breadcrumbs (p. 17) (⅓ cup)

½ teaspoon cinnamon

½ teaspoon ground ginger

500 g fresh or frozen rhubarb, cut into 1–2 cm (½ in) pieces* (about 4 ½–5 cups)

¼ cup sugar (50 g)

LIAISON:

2 large eggs

180 ml light cream (¾ cup)

3 tablespoons sugar

½ teaspoon vanilla extract or paste

*If you use frozen rhubarb, you will need to leave the tart in the oven for 45–50 minutes.

INSTRUCTIONS:

1. **Make the dough.** Whisk the flours together with the salt in a large bowl. Add the cold butter in pieces. Using a pastry blender or two knives, cut the butter into the flour mixture until it becomes the size of small pebbles. Make a well in the center and add the lightly beaten egg. Add 2 tablespoons of the water and stir everything together, just until a dough forms. Add up to another tablespoon of water if the dough is too dry. Shape the dough into a disk, wrap it in parchment paper and refrigerate for 30–60 minutes until it becomes firm.

2. Grease a 30 cm (11 ½ in) round tart pan. Take the dough out of the refrigerator and roll it out on the parchment paper it was wrapped in. Once you have a circle of dough large enough to fit the bottom and sides of the pan, place it with the parchment paper into the buttered tart pan. Press the dough into the bottom and sides of the pan. Using a fork, prick the bottom of the dough.

3. **Make the filling.** Whisk the breadcrumbs together with the cinnamon and ginger. Pour the mixture on top of the dough and spread it in an even layer. Then put the tart pan back in the refrigerator while you prepare the rest of the filling.

4. Add the rhubarb to a large bowl with the sugar and toss until well combined. Take the tart pan out of the refrigerator and spread the rhubarb and sugar mixture evenly on top.

5. **Make the liaison** (custard-like filling). In a large bowl, whisk the eggs, cream, sugar and vanilla together until well-blended. Pour the liaison evenly over the rhubarb.

6. Bake the tart on the bottom rack of a 180°C (350°F) oven for 35–45 minutes or until the liaison has set and the pastry has turned golden brown. Let the tart cool completely before serving.

A RHUBARB TART FOR SPRINGTIME

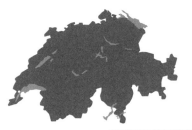

THROUGHOUT SWITZERLAND

Switzerland makes its fruit tarts flat and wide. Unlike fruit pies that I am used to in the US, Swiss tarts do not have a pastry lid. This allows you to see the beautiful colors of the fruit. It also reduces the ratio of pastry to filling, which makes the flavor of the fruit more prominent. These tarts sometimes have a liaison, also known as a *guélon* in French-speaking Switzerland. This egg and cream mixture, typically sweetened with sugar, is poured over the fruit before baking to create a custard-like filling.

One of my favorite seasonal tarts is made with rhubarb. In German, it is called a Rhabarberwähe, but I know it in French-speaking Switzerland as Tarte à la rhubarb. Given that rhubarb is technically a vegetable, it seems appropriate to serve this kind of tart for supper, even though it may still feel like a dessert.

I have added a layer of spiced breadcrumbs under the fruit and custard to my recipe. This helps absorb some of the moisture and prevents the bottom of the tart from becoming soggy. To make it a bit healthier, I use some whole wheat flour in the pastry dough and as little sugar as possible—just enough to counteract the sourness of the rhubarb.

The Vully region in the canton of Fribourg is particularly known for growing rhubarb—so much so that their reddish stalks have been included in the inventory of Switzerland's culinary heritage (*Patrimoine Culinaire Suisse*). The landscape that cascades around Mount Vully is well worth exploring for its vineyards and the scenic fields of rhubarb. Since you cannot find rhubarb all year round, its arrival in the springtime is a reason to celebrate—the perfect occasion for a suppertime tart!

51

TATSCH

CHOPPED PANCAKE WITH QUINCE PUREE

This super-quick chopped pancake from Graubünden works well for supper. I like serving it with a homemade quince puree, but you can also use your favorite applesauce. To make it a little sweeter, you can dust it with powdered sugar before serving.

Servings: 3–4

Prep: 10–15 mins
Cook: about 15 mins

INGREDIENTS:

125 g all-purpose flour (1 cup)

180 ml milk (¾ cup)

2 large eggs, separated into yolks and whites

zest ½ organic lemon (optional)

1 pinch of salt

2 tablespoons unsalted butter

INSTRUCTIONS:

1. Whisk the flour, milk, egg yolks and lemon zest together in a large bowl to form a batter. Set aside.

2. In another large bowl, add the egg whites and the salt. Use an electric mixer to beat the egg whites until they form stiff peaks. Gently fold the egg whites into the batter in the large bowl.

3. On the stove, melt 1 tablespoon of the butter in a large skillet over medium heat. Swirl the butter around the bottom and sides of the skillet. Pour in the batter and cook the pancake for 5–10 minutes until the bottom starts to lightly brown.

4. Cut the pancake into bite-size pieces with a spatula. Add the second tablespoon of butter to the pan and fry the pieces over medium-high heat, turning until they become lightly browned on all sides. Serve immediately with the quince puree (p. 238), stewed plums (p. 226) or applesauce.

QUINCE PUREE

Servings: 3–4

Prep: about 45 mins
Cook: 45–60 mins

INGREDIENTS:

1 teaspoon lemon juice

about 500 ml water (2 cups)

500 g quince (1 lb)

65 g sugar (⅓ cup)

INSTRUCTIONS:

1. In a medium saucepan, add the lemon juice and the water. Peel, halve, core and quarter the quinces, placing them immediately into the lemon water to prevent them from browning. When all the quinces are in the pan, add additional water so that they are just covered. Bring to a boil and simmer for 45–60 minutes until the quinces are soft. Take the pan off the heat and allow to cool.

2. When cooled, use an upright or immersion blender to puree the mixture until smooth. Add the sugar and return the pan to the stove over medium heat. Slowly heat the mixture to a simmer, stirring frequently until the sugar dissolves and the mixture thickens to the consistency of applesauce. Serve warm or cold.

Make-ahead tip:
When the puree is the consistency of applesauce, take the pan off the stove and transfer the puree to a heat-proof container. When it has cooled to room temperature, seal the container and refrigerate for up to 2–3 days.

GRAUBÜNDEN'S CHOPPED PANCAKE

CANTON
GRAUBÜNDEN

One summer when I was taking a cheesemaking class in Graubünden, I asked our instructor if he had ever made Tatsch. To my delight, he told me he had childhood memories of cooking it over a fire in the forest. This dish is just another example of a simple, rustic meal that you will find throughout Switzerland's Alpine regions.

You could describe Tatsch as a cross between a "Dutch baby" pancake and an American-style pancake, which is then chopped up. This sweet or sometimes savory dish comes from the canton of Graubünden. You probably already have all the ingredients in your pantry that you need to make it.

There are many ways to make this dish, as demonstrated by a 1905 cookbook from Chur that includes no fewer than seven recipes with Tatsch in the name. These recipes call for ingredients such as potatoes, apples and sour cream. The ultra-basic recipe for *Älplertatsch* only contains cream and flour, without listing any quantities, and describes cooking it over a fire and breaking the dough into smaller pieces.

Tatsch is quite similar to *Cholermus* from the canton of Obwalden. That dish is typically made with cream, like the old Churer recipe for *Älplertatsch*, but also includes eggs. Graubünden's chopped pancake is also reminiscent of *Kaiserschmarrn* from Austria, which translates to something like "emperor's mess."

I have made Tatsch outside in a cast iron pan on a grill and inside in a frying pan on the stove for supper with my family. It has become one of my go-to recipes when I have hungry people to feed, no matter what time of day.

TARTE AUX POIRES GENEVOISE

GENEVA PEAR TART

My version of a pear tart from Geneva works well for a sweet supper dish or dessert—or even breakfast! I recommend serving it while still a bit warm from the oven. A good accompaniment for this tart is a platter of cheese.

Servings: 4–6

Prep: 30–40 mins + 30–60 mins refrigeration
Bake: 35–45 mins

INGREDIENTS:

DOUGH:

150 g all-purpose flour
(1 ¼ cups)

1 pinch salt

75 g unsalted butter, cold
(⅓ cup)

60 ml tablespoons cold water
(¼ cup)

FILLING:

3 tablespoons raisins

1 tablespoon lemon juice

4–5 pears for baking, (e.g., Beurré Bosc or Williams) (750 g)

50 g sugar (¼ cup)

2 tablespoons all-purpose flour

½ teaspoon cinnamon

INSTRUCTIONS:

1. **Make the dough.** Whisk together the flour and salt in a large bowl. Add the cold butter and use a pastry blender or two knives to cut the butter into pieces the size of small pebbles. Make a well in the center and add the cold water. Stir everything together to form a dough. Shape the dough into a disk, wrap it in parchment paper and refrigerate it for 30–60 minutes.

2. When the dough has chilled, grease a 23–25 cm (9–10 in) tart pan, ideally with a removable bottom. Remove the dough from the parchment paper. Lay the sheet of parchment paper flat and dust it with flour. Dust a rolling pin with flour and roll out the dough until you have a circle large enough to fit the bottom and sides of the pan. If you are using a non-stick pan with a removable bottom, invert the dough into the pan. Otherwise, press the sheet of parchment paper with the dough on it into the pan. Fold in or cut off any excess dough from the sides of the pan. Then use a fork to prick the bottom of the dough in several places. Place the tart pan in the refrigerator to chill until the filling is ready.

3. **Make the filling.** Add the raisins and lemon juice to a large bowl. Peel, halve and core the pears. Slice into thin pieces and cut these pieces in half. Add them to the bowl immediately and toss in the juice to prevent

them from turning brown. When all the pears are in the bowl, add the sugar, flour and cinnamon and gently mix until well combined.

4. **Make the tart.** Take the tart pan out of the fridge. Add the pear filling, spreading it evenly and making sure the raisins are well-distributed. Bake at 200°C (400°F) on the bottom rack of the oven for 35–45 minutes until the pears have softened and the crust has lightly browned. Let the tart cool in the pan for about 10 minutes before transferring it to a wire rack. Serve warm or at room temperature.

GENEVA'S WINTER PEAR TART

CANTON GENEVE

You may already be familiar with Geneva's famous plum tart, baked for the annual Jeûne Genevois (Geneva's fasting day). This cantonal holiday takes place the Thursday after the first Sunday in September. Baked because plums are in season that time of year, people relied on plum tarts to break their fast. The tarts could be made in advance, so people could spend the day in church.

Not only do the Genevois love their plums, but during the city's annual Fête de l'Escalade and the end-of year holiday season, you will also find specialties made with pears. You can read more about the Fête de l'Escalade in the story that accompanies the recipe for Soupe de la Mère Royaume (p. 59). The pear specialties made during winter include Rissoles aux poires (spiced pear hand pies) and Tarte aux poires (pear tart).

The FRUCTUS association based in Wädenswil (Zurich) works to support the preservation of old and sometimes forgotten fruit varieties, including pears. According to FRUCTUS, you can find more than 600 different varieties of pears in Switzerland, including Williams (Valais), Culotte Suisse (Neuchâtel), Botzi (Fribourg) and Rissole (Geneva). The Rissole pear, also known as Marlioz, gets its name from its use in Rissoles aux poires.

When you make Geneva's Tarte aux poires, I recommend using a pear variety with a firm texture that is suitable for baking. In Switzerland, pear varieties such as Beurré Bosc or Williams are good choices. Several recipes for this tart call for the addition of candied citrus peel, but I have opted not to include it in my recipe, to focus the flavor of the tart on the pears and to make it a little less sweet for suppertime.

IX.
ACKNOWLEDGEMENTS

To create a cookbook like this requires the help of so many people. Throughout my time in Switzerland, I have received thoughtful contributions from generous individuals who have shared their cookbooks, stories and expertise with me. It would be impossible to name all the people who have guided me and influenced my work along the way. Sometimes, a five-minute conversation years ago in a bakery or a restaurant sparked an idea that eventually turned into a recipe.

When I started writing this cookbook, my immediate family—Nate, Augustus and Hendrik—were my first and most important sounding boards and critics. If they did not like a recipe, then it did not go into the book—with some exceptions of course for personal preferences. They helped consume all my creations—good or bad!

Next, I must thank my favorite French photographer, Dorian Rollin, who I got to work with for the third time. Together with the endlessly creative food stylist, Camille Stoos, we spent two very productive long weekends cooking and photographing the dishes for this cookbook. I am a terribly serious person, so I enjoy spending time with these two people who always make me laugh—especially during those moments when the pressure is on to take the perfect shot. I am grateful to my publisher, Helvetiq, for bringing us together again.

Speaking of Helvetiq, I am especially thankful for their investment in this cookbook and for continuing to support my work. A huge thanks to Hadi Barkat for his vision and enthusiasm, and to my project manager, Myriam Sauter, whose positive attitude always carried me through. And, what a pleasure it was to work with the talented editor, Leah Witton, who helped make my writing so much stronger! I am also thrilled with the eye-catching illustrations by our impressive graphic designer, Jagna Pilczuk.

Special thanks are especially due to my dear sister, Mara Nieuwsma. She read every word in every chapter early on and gave me honest feedback like only a sister could. And to my mother, who was responsible for making all our suppers when we were growing up—I appreciate her hard work cooking for us now more than ever.

Likewise, to all the people who agreed to test my recipes, I cannot thank you enough: Kate Allen & Curtis Moore, David Anchel, Susannah Bloch, Koenraad De Vylder, Jen Estigoy, Claire Fitzpatrick, Louise Kasser Genecand, Elizabeth Gonzalez, James Gosteli, Helen Kim, Nicole Klauss, Joan

Sullivan Mahagan, Jeana Marshak, Susan & Olivier Merkt, Stephen & Amantha Moore, the Mostoller family, Melayna Nieuwsma, Laure Niquille Rahman, Michael Nunn, Pauline Persoud, Susan Renna, Jennifer Robertson, Samantha Rousseau, Jonathan Seigel, Ashley Schütz, Molly Schuetze, Salina Swanson, Julie Walder, and Jessica Zeuli. Your feedback helped to ensure that others will be successful in making these dishes at home.

In terms of research for this book, I want to thank Dominik Flammer for letting me peruse and borrow several excellent books from his personal collection. Swiss libraries and librarians have also provided invaluable assistance: Delphine Bongard (Bibliothèque de Genève), Barbara Vonlanthen (Kantonsbibliothek Thurgau, Frauenfeld), the Swiss National Library (Bern), and the Mediatheque/Mediathek Valais. In addition, Swiss tourism offices have provided helpful assistance in tracking down some of the regional dishes. A big thanks to Conny Baer and Chiara Iotti (Obwalden Tourismus) and Patricia Krüsi (St.Gallen-Bodensee Tourismus). Swiss museum staff also contributed time and research help: Sophia Aschwanden (Historisches Museum Luzern) and Mark Bertogliati (Museo etnografico della Valle di Muggio). I need to say thanks as well to research assistance provided by Mathieu Avanzi, Brigitt Flüeler, Ursula Käser, Karl Wimmer and Franco Lurà. The following people who helped review sections of the book also deserve recognition: Frédéric Auderset, Yoyo Bischofberger, Bernadette Bissig, Caroline Chapuis, Sherly Cho, Roman Diethelm, Arnaud & Jennifer Favre, Léandre & Johanna Guillod, Renata Neukom, Marylise Walder, Thalia Wünsche, and Nancy Wolf.

Finally, I want to express my immense gratitude for the in-kind support from Stiftung Ferien im Baudenkmal. This foundation is committed to the preservation of historic properties throughout Switzerland. They work to help save heritage sites that might otherwise be destroyed due to neglect or economic pressure for redevelopment. As a result, these properties are reinvented as one-of-a-kind vacation apartments and homes. You can stay in the properties, sleep in their cozy bedrooms and cook in their kitchens, imagining what life must have been like for earlier generations.

Just as with our previous partnerships for the *Swiss Bread* and *Sweet + Swiss* cookbooks, Stiftung Ferien im Baudenkmal once again allowed us to use their historic properties as a backdrop for the photographs in this book. We had the opportunity to stay at two of their properties, starting with the Taunerhaus, a small farmhouse built in 1850 in Vinelz (Bern), near the shores of Lake Biel/Bienne. Our wonderful hosts, Romina and Florian, made us feel right at home. We then traveled to the Kaplanei in Ernen (Valais) in early spring. After being vacant for over 70 years, the foundation breathed new life into this former rectory. The elegant stone building has a chapel, rococo ceiling paintings and baroque wall paneling. I am indebted to my friend Jennifer Abell who assisted me during this second photo shoot. She also provided critical moral support when my Rösti dramatically fell onto the floor! As in previous years, the time I spent in these two remarkable properties with Dorian and Camille will not be forgotten. I loved bringing traditional Swiss recipes to these historic sites.

For more information
Stiftung Ferien im Baudenkmal
Zollikerstrasse 128
8008 Zurich
+41 (0)44 252 28 72
info@fib.ch
ferienimbaudenkmal.ch

RECIPE CLASSIFICATION

RECIPES BY GEOGRAPHIC AREA

INDEX